POPULAR
MUSIC

The Popular Music Series

Popular Music, 1920-1979 is a revised cumulation of and supersedes Volumes 1 through 8 of the *Popular Music* series, of which Volumes 3 through 8 are still available:

Popular Music, 1900-1919 is a new, companion volume to the revised cumulation. This series continues with:

Other Books by Bruce Pollock

In Their Own Words: Popular Songwriting, 1955-1974

The Face of Rock and Roll: Images of a Generation

When Rock Was Young: The Heyday of Top 40

When the Music Mattered: Rock in the 1960s

ISSN 0886-442X

VOLUME 15
1990

POPULAR MUSIC

An Annotated Guide to American Popular Songs,
Including Introductory Essay, Lyricists and Composers
Index, Important Performances Index, Awards Index,
and List of Publishers

BRUCE POLLOCK
Editor

 Gale Research Inc. · *DETROIT* · *LONDON*

7

Bruce Pollock, *Editor*
Barbara Beals, *Editorial Assistant*

Mary Beth Trimper, *Production Manager*
Deborah L. Milliken, *External Production Assistant*

Arthur Chartow, *Art Director*
C.J. Jonik, *Keyliner*
Yolanda Y. Latham, *Keyliner*

Dennis LaBeau, *Editorial Data Systems Director*
Theresa Rocklin, *Program Design*
Benita L. Spight, *Data Entry Supervisor*
Edgar Jackson, *Data Entry Associate*

Lawrence W. Baker, *Editor, Popular Music Series*

The paper used in this publication meets the minimum requirements
of American National Standard for Information Sciences—Permanence
Paper for Printed Library Materials, ANSI Z39.48-1984. ∞™

Library of Congress Catalog Card Number 85-653754
ISBN 0-8103-4947-7
ISSN 0886-442X

Published simultaneously in the United Kingdom
by Gale Research International Limited
(An affiliated company of Gale Research Inc.)

Contents

About the Book and
How to Use It

This volume is the fifteenth of a series whose aim is to set down in permanent and practical form a selective, annotated list of the significant popular songs of our times. Other indexes of popular music have either dealt with special areas, such as jazz or theater and film music, or been concerned chiefly with songs that achieved a degree of popularity as measured by the music-business trade indicators, which vary widely in reliability.

Annual Publication Schedule

The first nine volumes in the *Popular Music* series covered sixty-five years of song history in increments of five or ten years. Volume 10 initiated a new annual publication schedule, making background information available as soon as possible after a song achieves prominence. Yearly publication also allows deeper coverage—over five hundred songs this year, instead of about three hundred, with additional details about writers' inspiration, uses of songs, album appearances, and more. (Songs with copyright dates before 1990 have full entries in this volume if not covered in the series before. Cross references lead to complete entries in earlier volumes for songs already prominent in previous years.)

Indexes Provide Additional Access

Three indexes make the valuable information in the song listings even more accessible to users. The Lyricists & Composers Index shows all the songs represented in *Popular Music, 1990,* that are credited to a given individual. The Important Performances Index (introduced in the revised cumulation, *Popular Music, 1920-1979*) tells at a glance what albums, musicals, films, television shows, or other media featured songs are represented in the volume. The "Performer" category—first added to the index as "Vocalist" in the 1986 volume—allows the user to see with what songs an artist has been associated this year. The index is arranged by broad media category, then alphabetically by the show or album title, with the songs listed under each title. Finally, the Awards Index (also introduced in the cumulation) provides a list of the songs nominated for awards by the American Academy of Motion Picture Arts and Sciences (Academy Award) and the American Academy of Recording Arts and Sciences (Grammy Award). Winning songs are indicated by asterisks.

About the Book and How to Use It

List of Publishers

The List of Publishers is an alphabetically arranged directory providing addresses for the publishers of the songs represented in this fifteenth volume of Popular Music. Also noted is the organization handling performance rights for the publisher—American Society of Composers, Authors, and Publishers (ASCAP), Broadcast Music, Inc. (BMI), or Society of European Stage Authors and Composers (SESAC).

Tracking Down Information on Songs

Unfortunately, the basic records kept by the active participants in the music business are often casual, inaccurate, and transitory. There is no single source of comprehensive information about popular songs, and those sources that do exist do not publish complete material about even the musical works with which they are directly concerned. Two of the primary proprietors of basic information about our popular music are the major performing rights societies—ASCAP and BMI. Although each of these organizations has considerable information about the songs of its own writer and publisher members and has also issued indexes of its own songs, their files and published indexes are designed primarily for clearance identification by the commercial users of music. Their publications of annual or periodic lists of their "hits" necessarily include only a small fraction of their songs, and the facts given about these are also limited. Both ASCAP and BMI are, however, invaluable and indispensable sources of data about popular music. It is just that their data and special knowledge are not readily accessible to the researcher.

Another basic source of information about musical compositions and their creators and publishers is the Copyright Office of the Library of Congress. There a computerized file lists each published, unpublished, republished, and renewed copyright of songs registered with the Office since 1979. This is helpful for determining the precise date of the declaration of the original ownership of musical works, but contains no other information. To complicate matters further, some authors, composers, and publishers have been known to employ rather makeshift methods of protecting their works legally, and there are songs listed in Popular Music that may not be found in the Library of Congress files.

Selection Criteria

In preparing this series, the editor was faced with a number of separate problems. The first and most important of these was that of selection. The stated aim of the project—to offer the user as comprehensive and accurate a listing of significant popular songs as possible—has been the guiding criterion. The purpose has never been to offer a judgment on the quality of any songs or to indulge a prejudice for or against any type of popular music. Rather, it is the purpose of *Popular Music* to document those musical works that (1) achieved a substantial degree of popular acceptance, (2) were exposed to the public in especially notable circumstances, or (3) were accepted and given important performances by influential musical and dramatic artists.

Another problem was whether or not to classify the songs as to type. Most works of music are subject to any number of interpretations and, although it is possible to describe a particular performance, it is more difficult to give a musical composition a label applicable not only to its origin but to its subsequent musical history. In fact, the most significant versions of some songs are often quite at variance with their origins. Citations for such songs in *Popular Music* indicate the important facts about not only their origins but also their subsequent lives, rather than assigning an arbitrary and possibly misleading label.

Research Sources

The principal sources of information for the titles, authors, composers, publishers, and dates of copyright of the songs in this volume were the Copyright Office of the Library of Congress, ASCAP, BMI, and individual writers and publishers. Data about best-selling recordings were obtained principally from two of the leading music business trade journals—*Billboard* and *Cash Box*. For the historical notes; information about foreign, folk, public domain, and classical origins; and identification of theatrical, film, and television introducers of songs, the editor relied upon collections of album notes, theater programs, sheet music, newspaper and magazine articles, and other material, both his own and that in the Lincoln Center Library for the Performing Arts in New York City.

Contents of a Typical Entry

The primary listing for a song includes

- Title and alternate title(s)
- Country of origin (for non-U.S. songs)
- Author(s) and composer(s)
- Current publisher, copyright date
- Annotation on the song's origins or performance history

Title: The full title and alternate title or titles are given exactly as they appear on the Library of Congress copyright record or, in some cases, the sheet music. Since even a casual perusal of the book reveals considerable variation in spelling and punctuation, it should be noted that these are the colloquialisms of the music trade. The title of a given song as it appears in this series is, in almost all instances, the one under which it is legally registered.

About the Book and How to Use It

Foreign Origin: If a song is of foreign origin, the primary listing indicates the country of origin after the title. Additional information may be noted, such as the original title, copyright date, writer, publisher in country of origin, or other facts about the adaptation.

Authorship: In all cases, the primary listing reports the author or authors and the composer or composers. The reader may find variations in the spelling of a songwriter's name. This results from the fact that some writers used different forms of their names at different times or in connection with different songs. These variants appear in the Lyricists & Composers Index as well. In addition to this kind of variation in the spelling of writers' names, the reader will also notice that in some cases, where the writer is also the performer, the name as a writer may differ from the form of the name used as a performer.

Publisher: The current publisher is listed. Since *Popular Music* is designed as a practical reference work rather than an academic study, and since copyrights more than occasionally change hands, the current publisher is given instead of the original holder of the copyright. If a publisher has, for some reason, copyrighted a song more than once, the years of the significant copyright subsequent to the year of the original copyright are also listed after the publisher's name.

Annotation: The primary listing mentions significant details about the song's history—the musical, film, or other production in which the song was introduced or featured and, where important, by whom it was introduced, in the case of theater and film songs; any other performers identified with the song; first or best-selling recordings and album inclusions, indicating the performer and the record company; awards; and other relevant data. The name of a performer may be listed differently in connection with different songs, especially over a period of years. The name listed is the form of the name given in connection with a particular performance or record. It should be noted that the designation "best-selling record" does not mean that the record was a "hit." It means simply that the record or records noted as "best-selling" were the best-selling record or records of that particular song, in comparison with the sales of other records of the same song. Dates are provided for important recordings and performances.

Cross-References

Any alternate titles appearing in bold type after the main title in a primary listing are also cross-referenced in the song listings. If a song previously covered in the *Popular Music* series also attained prominence in 1990, the title and new achievement are noted here with a reference to the appropriate earlier volume.

Popular Music in 1990

It is a truism unique to popular music that whenever a particularly static, bland, conservative, or uneventful period of record-making settles in for an extended length of time, the popular taste reverts to black music to fill the void. This is not so surprising, when you consider that black music is where rock 'n' roll started, when rhythm & blues erupted from the black teenage subculture in the '50s to provide whites with the innovation, the inspiration, and the impetus to recreate it in their own, more palatable image. But, ironically, the observation is usually unfavorable, indicating a momentary lull in the action, when music in general has lost its focus, when the naked beat has prevailed above all else, when lyrics have fallen out of fashion, and causes have lost their constituencies. And, more to the point, when there is no galvanizing white male force to bring others up the pop charts with him. In this context, the truism concludes, similarly clad, faceless black acts are free to clutter the musical airspace, with nothing heavier on their minds than the beat, no agenda but the exploitation of a basic sexuality that precedes rhythm & blues, to the blues root from which all that has followed it has sprung.

Thus, there is a precedent for the dominance in 1990 of black acts and black music crossing from the rhythm & blues chart to the dance floors of America, from Snap to Seduction to Stevie B. What is fairly *un*precedented, however, is that black music and its various offshoots dominated 1990 as no other year in recent history. The lyrics and concerns of this music came of age, maturing and evolving into an art form that encompassed virtually every important aspect of the year in popular song, from the serious to the sublime, from the revolutionary to the ridiculous, from Public Enemy's pronouncements like "Welcome to the Terrordome," "Revolutionary Generation," "Fear of a Black Planet," "Burn Hollywood Burn," and "Brothers Gonna Work It Out," to their opposite, more visible and controversial, but ultimately less threatening counterpart, the 2 Live Crew, with "Banned in the USA" and "Arrest in Effect," detailing their life and times in the forefront of 1990's censorship travails. With rap groups like these, and hundreds of others in between, making news with their use of the language for the purpose of expressing sentiments that are not G-rated, once again music became dangerous, reaching for a volatile vitality not heard in years.

Popular Music in 1990

The Many Styles of Black Music Dominate the Pop Scene

But black music was about more than threatening sentiments this year. It was also about achievements past and steps ahead. It moved into multimedia exposure with unprecedented strength, celebrating its history and diversity with admirable effect. Spike Lee, about as visible a black culture icon as there is these days, was responsible for two of the finest moments. Featured in his film *Mo' Better Blues*, the rap "A Jazz Thing," by Gangstarr, offered a concise and passionate history and defense of jazz, in poetry as profound as any beatnik mantra, from Charlie Parker to John Coltrane to Wynton and Branford Marsalis (Branford co-composed the piece). At the other end of the musical and media spectrum, Lee produced a TV special called *Do It a Cappella*, in which the Persuasions, long keepers of the do-wop flame, came forward with their signature tune "Looking for an Echo," to poignantly evoke the heyday of rock's golden age of rhythm & blues. Another widely noted event of the year was the release of the complete recordings of the noted Delta bluesman Robert Johnson. To see his boxed CD set, containing such legendary tunes as "Me and the Devil Blues," "Phonograph Blues," and "If I Had Possession over Judgment Day," scaling album charts and sparking a blues revival in young musicians, black and white, was to experience the kind of epiphany early exponents of rhythm & blues might have felt when hearing their music surge up from underground to dominate the '50s. Capping a proud year, Melba Moore joined some famous friends to bring a revival of the Negro national anthem, "Lift Every Voice and Sing," to the charts once more.

From the high tech wizardry of Digital Underground's "The Humpty Dance," to the street-honed mesmerizing rap genius of A Tribe Called Quest, in "I Left My Wallet in El Segundo," to Brenda Fassie's tribute to her uncle Nelson Mandela, "Black President," this was music as serious as it had to be. At the same time, it was danceable, as Janet Jackson proved by sending five tunes from her *Rhythm Nation 1814* album to the upper reaches of the charts, among them "Escapade," "Alright," and "Come Back to Me," all co-written with Terry Lewis and James Harris. Kenny Edmunds, also known as Babyface, had another banner year, solo and with L.A. Reid and sometimes Darryl Simmons, writing tunes for his own album and others', among them "Can't Stop," "I'm Your Baby Tonight," "My Kinda Girl," "Giving You the Benefit," "Ready or Not," "Tender Lover," and "Whip Appeal."

Popular acclaim and across-the-board success were never a stranger to Quincy Jones, long a mentor and innovator in the field. His efforts this year for the LP *Back on the Block* were rewarded with a Grammy. Prince's film and album *Graffiti Bridge* continued his irrepressible saga. Although the influential Curtis Mayfield's comeback collaboration with rapper Ice-T, in "Superfly 1990," was tragically aborted when a freak stage accident left him paralyzed, we did see in 1990 all-time blues great Willie Dixon surface in collaboration with Cesar Rosas of Los Lobos in "I Can't Understand."

The complex issue of sampling rose to the fore this year, merging black music, dance music, technology, and history, symbolized by M.C. Hammer's major smash "U Can't Touch This," which was based on Rick James' track for his 1981 hit "Super Freak." As publishers, commentators, record labels, and artists past and present continue to debate the legal, creative, ethical, and financial ramifications of sampling others' works, en toto or in part, for use in new works, the technique itself marches to its own dancing drummer, defying logic and the law as it produces award-winning hits in new collagelike works as powerful as any in the history of popular music, as well as in abjectly pilfered works, as derivative and banal as they are offensive.

In the meantime, the trickle-down effect of this black abundance was immediately picked up on in the nightlife of Middle America. Just as the nation's favorite dance instructor, Paula Abdul, was finishing off her 1989 album with her 1990 hit "Opposites Attract," the anything-goes atmosphere produced its share of strange bedfellows, from the inspired white fruitcake of Was (Not Was) merging with the classic rhythm & blues of The Temptations in "Papa Was a Rolling Stone," to the dour Suzanne Vega having her 1987 tone poem, "Tom's Diner," turned into a pumped-up disco smash by an outfit called DNA (breath of life, indeed!). How about the spectre of square-jawed Robbie Van Winkle, posing as Vanilla Ice, borrowing the Queen/David Bowie groove from "Under Pressure" for his monumentally successful "Ice Ice Baby," in perhaps the most calculated "Elvis-Presley-white-boy-who-can-sing-and-move-like-a-black-boy" ploy since Ral Donner? Producer Maurice Starr came up with a separate but equal answer to his own opposite marketing question with The New Kids on the Block: "If I could get five white boys who sing and move like white boys trying to be black, I might have the white Jackson Five."

Is it any wonder then, that black's new and thus far only heavy metal hope, Living Colour, would choose this year to proclaim, in their diatribe against a white culture that has lived off the legend and works of the black culture for most of its lifespan, drawing sustenance and chord changes, that "Elvis Is Dead?"

Kids Get Up and Dance

But in the discos of New York and elsewhere, kids were too busy dancing to contemplate the implications of such cross-cultural co-mingling. Spear-headed by the delovely Miss Kier, Deeelite's encounter with Herbie Hancock resulted in the dance sensation that swept the nation, "Groove Is in the Heart." Though widely touted as a psychedelic throwback, Deeelite's nearest and dearest influence was probably the much more recent B-52's, the beloved beehived troupe out of Athens, Georgia, who came out of itchy-kitschy oblivion in 1989 to have a landmark year, represented in 1990 with "Roam." From Europe, the contributions of two white females were acknowledged on the jittery dance floors of America. The girl with the curl, Lisa Stansfield, had an international smash with "All Around the World," while her opposite number, the girl with the crewcut, Sinead O'Connor, took on an old Prince tune, "Nothing Compares 2 U," and by all reports, fought his Royal Badness to a draw. New York City's Mariah Carey, product of a mixed marriage of pop and rhythm & blues, offered us her pipes and her compelling "Vision of Love," while in England, a genuinely psychedelic dance movement was afoot, with bands like Happy Mondays, Inspiral Carpets, and, especially, 808 State offering a peppy alternative to the mopey sounds of Depeche Mode ("Policy of Truth," "Enjoy the Silence," "Personal Jesus") and The Cure ("Pictures of You"), completing transatlantic dance break throughs this year. At the other end of the black-based music spectrum entirely, old man Mose Allison kept on rolling along, as remarkable and self-effacing as ever in "Ever Since I Stole the Blues."

The Milli Vanilli Saga

With all the flash and glitter, whirling strobes, and artificially enhanced, computer-generated, techno-synthesized big beats getting bigger all the time, it came as something of a surprise when the pop community suddenly chose to take huge affront this year with poor Milli Vanilli, when, for some unknown reason, it was revealed that they did not, in fact, sing on any of their hit records. Though rock 'n' roll has a long history of such shenanigans, smilingly overlooked by insiders and outsiders alike, this was the year the people at the Grammys decided to strip the group of its 1989 award for Best New Artist. Certainly the committee was embarrassed over the gaffe, though not nearly as embarrassed as they should have been for having bestowed the award on such a dreadfully incompetent act in the first place; yet all the righteous hoopla, the charges and counter-charges back and forth, only served to fuel the cynics among us into thoughts that this was but a prelude to a comeback of the new, improved Milli Vanilli, with the real singers being introduced, whoever they may be, or whoever the producers might dredge up this time, and the old, disgraced Milli Vanillis, Rob and Fab, getting a good old American Second Chance with a new album, complete with their own improved, artificially enhanced, computer-generated, techno-synthesized new voices. In the end, who cares anyway? Especially in the studio of the '90s, where you can dress anything up to look like Julia Roberts in *Pretty Woman* or, at least, Michelangelo in *Teenage Mutant Ninja Turtles, Part Five*. Nevertheless, with the litigious '80s turning into the moralizing '90s, a backlash against such fakery may be taking hold, as evidence by the erstwhile

Weather Girl, Martha Wash, who got out her datebook and her contact lenses to discover herself listed as the singer on the sessions for a number of dance hits credited to other people, chief among them Black Box's "Everybody Everything." The year ended with the record's producers claiming it was a misunderstanding and Wash looking forward to proper remuneration. It's a long way from the legendary Darlene Love, the Martha Wash of the early '60s, who sang without credit on all those hits by The Crystals.

What shouldn't be discounted in the whole Milli Vanilli flap, when all is said and done, are the quality tunes put out under that assumed moniker, most provided by pop's reigning pen, Diane Warren. Her apt eulogy for her top client's career, "All or Nothing," was only part of her own scintillating year, in which "I'll Be Your Shelter," "Your Baby Never Looked Good in Blue," "Love Will Lead You Back," "When I'm Back on My Feet Again," and "How Can We Be Lovers" all occupied much psychic room at the Inn of Popular Subconsciousness. This last title was perhaps *the* professional's professional song of the year, a collaboration not only with singer Michael Bolton, who had been the journeyman's journeyman until last year's breakthrough, but also with Desmond Child, the noted song doctor, who has seemingly written at least a piece of every third hard rock band's current anthem, from Kiss to Bon Jovi to Aerosmith to Poison.

Musical Consciousness: From Patriotism to the Environment

Apart from professionalism, pop's prevailing cause this year was the budding war in the Persian Gulf, which spawned several hit songs, while freedom in Eastern Europe, symbolized by the fall of the Berlin Wall, led only to a superstar concert performance of Pink Floyd's 1980 epic, *The Wall*. Julie Gold's "From a Distance," although discovered (and co-published) by Nanci Griffith in 1987, became an anthem for our troops in 1990 (and the Grammy-winning Song of the Year) by virtue of its big Bette Midler treatment (the same kind that turned "The Wind Beneath My Wings" into a mega-hit after a hundred others had failed to do so. When is Bette going to do the same for Randy Newman's "I Think It's Going to Rain Today?"). Also big among patriotic radio programmers were George Michael's "Praying for Time" and, at the redneck end of the spectrum, Hank Williams Jr.'s prescient "Don't Give Us a Reason."

For the most part, however, Top 40 radio was more interested in purveying a white bread vision of harmony to its teenage constituency, with show-biz kids like Wilson Phillips ("Hold On," "Release Me") and Nelson ("Love and Affection") calling the tune. The slightly naughty "Cherry Pie," by Warrant, only affirmed the neutered sensuality of an era dominated by Madonna's "Hanky Panky"; her posing histrionics in "Vogue" and "Justify My Love" were about as steamy as a typical TV movie of the week—but with much higher ratings. About the only breakthrough of a true adolescent outside sensibility into the fearful, placid, kinder-and-gentler mind-set of the average pop listener was accomplished by Faith No More, with their pitiful rallying cry "You want it all but you can't have it" certainly more reality-based than The Doors' Jim Morrison's long-ago preening "We want the world and we want it now!"

A more potent read on the subliminal consciousness of the popular (white) audience can be gleaned from inspecting the various ready-to-eat chunks into which pop and pop radio have been broken for consumer consumption like separate compartments on a TV dinner tray. Rather than railing against such discriminatory practices, however, music fans in the '90s may find new freedom in this kind of narrow casting. Freed from the tyranny of having to be everything to everyone, radio stations can go deeper into their chosen style of music to the exclusion of distracting factions—not that they do. But listeners can sample tunes from a dozen genres just by pushing buttons, moving from hard rock to acoustic folk, from new age and country music to experimental psychedelic dance and garage bands on the fringes of industrial white noise.

Thus, the musical spectrum of a given night in 1990 included Bruce Hornsby taking on the Ku Klux Klan in "Fire on the Cross." Neil Young sang of saving the planet in "Mother Earth," as did Michelle Shocked in the swinging "On the Greener Side." Even the childrens' singer Raffi contributed a tune to this year's most pressing environmental issue, "Big Beautiful Planet." The legacy of Phil Ochs was illuminated somewhere on the dial, when They Might Be Giants revived "One More Parade" and British folksinger Billy Bragg recorded "I Dreamed I Saw Phil Ochs Last Night," set to the tune of the old labor hymn "I Dreamed I Saw Joe Hill," which Ochs as well as Joan Baez popularized in the bygone radical '60s. Bemoaning the lack of similar commitment in today's generation, John Hiatt offered the powerful "Through Your Hands," and Canadian folksinger Ferron the emotional "Stand Up (Love in the Corners)." Irish singer/songwriter Karl Wallinger answered them with the staunch credo "Ain't Gonna Come Till I'm Ready," while the metal band Suicidal Tendencies spoke for the many who can't find their music anywhere on radio or MTV, with the angry "You Can't Bring Me Down." The acerbic Loudon Wainwright summed up the repressive atmosphere with "Jesse Don't Like It," dedicated to Senator Jesse Helms and the whole censorship issue, which, ironically, could be just the stimulation the rock constituency needs to kick itself into some kind of moral and artistic gear for the rest of the decade (though I'm not sure Wainwright is precisely the white singer around which a major stylistic and seismic shift could ever coalesce).

Then again, it probably won't be Bruce Springsteen either, as evidenced by what was on his mind when he took the stage at a benefit performance in

California this year, to showcase some new tunes called "Real World," "The Wish," "When the Lights Go Out," and "57 Channels (and Nothin' On)." Obviously, he's fighting off the same terminal couch potato malaise as many in the generation, epitomized as well by They Might Be Giants ("Whistling in the Dark," "Someone Keeps Moving My Chair") and Bob Dylan's pet project, the Traveling Wilburys, which was predominated by claustrophobic complaints like "Upside Down" and the hilarious "Cool Dry Place." Paul Simon did manage to get out of the house, but had to leave the country for Brazil to find the inspiration for *The Rhythm of the Saints*, much as he went to Africa for *Graceland*.

Though some ethnic bonding might entice someone to partake of the neighborhoods evoked by Los Lobos ("The Neighborhood") in the west and The Silos ("Pictures of Helen") in the east, or even The Indigo Girls ("Southland in the Springtime"), for the most part, fear and trembling stalked the urban landscape and its people, places, and, especially, interpersonal relationships. Moe Berg in the Canadian band Pursuit of Happiness charted the post-sexual revolution in "Shave Your Legs," while folk music's answer to Judith Viorst, Christine Lavin, added to the prevailing male-female angst in "Sensitive New Age Guys." Hard rock's reigning bad boys, Guns N' Roses, singing at the Farm Aid benefit, debuted a searing lament called "Civil War," which, considering their past predilection for gay- and race-baiting, could certainly be taken on many levels. Nineteen ninety also marked the return of those fiendish proto-techno-punks from Akron, known as Devo, whose "Post Post Modern Man" successfully contributed to the anxious zeitgeist. Even more dire in their musical persona was the atonal energy of Sonic Youth, going almost pop with "Kool Thing" and "Cinderella's Big Score." It's a wonder, in this bleak atmosphere, where almost every other band, from Aerosmith to The Black Crowes, was singing some form of the blues, that Lonesome Val had the wherewithal to conceive of the fervently optimistic "To Be Young."

Rock Eulogies

Of course, there were many reasons to treasure the breathing of each breath in 1990, as usual brought on by tragedy. The long-awaited album by the blues guitar-playing Vaughan Brothers from Austin, Texas, Jimmie and Stevie Ray, received much more attention than it might have, due to its release just after Stevie Ray's demise in a plane crash. In that grim context, virtually all of its tunes sounded like eulogies. It was a eulogy, as well, that brought out the best in former rock 'n' roll partners Lou Reed and John Cale, once of the powerful and influential Velvet Underground, when they debuted their thirteen-song tone poem of tribute to Andy Warhol in 1989. This year it came out in recorded form as *Songs for Drella*, one of the most personal and important works ever created for mass consumption, with such songs as "Smalltown," "The Trouble with Classicists," "Faces and Names," "Forever

Changed," and the poignant farewell "Hello It's Me," charting the life and death not only of their founder and mentor but of a downtown art and music era. To further establish this profound work's importance, all thirteen songs are included in this volume of *Popular Music*, to encourage other such elaborate songwriting ventures in the future.

Something of this nature is what popular song aficionados have long envisioned as a direction that might be taken up by the musical theater, utilizing the talents of artists like Reed and Cale, Paul Simon, Randy Newman, Leonard Cohen, Bruce Springsteen, Bob Dylan, Suzanne Vega, or Joni Mitchell, as well as Craig Carnelia, William Finn, Stephen Sondheim, Richard Maltby, or David Shire, in the service of a subject so inspired that the resulting work would validate the moldering presence of musical theater in America. Instead, this year we got a glitzy presentation of the Buddy Holly catalogue.

TV, Theater, and Film Highlights

With songs so omnipresent in movie soundtracks and unavoidable as self-conscious mini-dramas on MTV, the impact of an individual song has been ridiculously diluted, yet, when the right combination of words and music comes along on the larger-than-life mediums of TV or film, its effect is undeniable. David Lynch proved this with his moody subterranean soundtrack to *Twin Peaks*, a kind of *West Side Story* by way of *A Summer Place*, composed by Angelo Badalamenti, complete with Duane Eddy-like twangy guitar and vocals by Julee Cruise more breathless than the Fleetwoods. If no hit songs came from that show, Lynch was at least responsible for Chris Isaak's haunting post-rockabilly version of "Wicked Game," which started its journey to hit status in Lynch's 1990 movie *Wild at Heart*. On the other hand, despite a theme song provided by Randy Newman ("Under the Gun") and notable staff-produced epics every week by the likes of Amanda "The Rose" McBroom, and others, the TV sing 'em up, so-called rock opera, *Cop Rock*, died a merciful death before the fat lady even had a chance to sing. (Coincidentally, one fat lady who *did* get a chance to sing on television, comedienne Roseanne Barr, certainly made the most of it, parlaying her spirited off-key rendition of "The Star Spangled Banner" into an album named for its first single, "I Enjoy Being a Girl.")

Meanwhile, not necessarily operating at a significantly higher level on the show-biz scale, Mssrs. Rado, Ragni, and MacDermot, authors once upon a time of the first—and probably last—successful rock opera, *Hair*, were back on the boards at a New York cabaret, trying out tunes called "Wow," "Planet Love," and "Absolutely Swing," for a new play entitled *Sun*. Of course, in the realms of theatrical kitsch, these fellows still have a long way to travel before they can match *The Rocky Horror Picture Show*. As a testament to the longevity of this midnight exercise in high camp, an album came out this year not only commemorating the show's magnificent run, but putting in some never before and rarely heard Richard O'Brian tunes like "Sword of Damocles," "Planet Schmanet Janet," and "Once in a While."

More mainstream were the activities of Charles Strouse and Richard Maltby, unveiling some tunes from *Nick and Nora*, and Rupert Holmes polishing *Swing*. Its opening delayed by casting complications, *Miss Saigon* nevertheless released its English cast album over here; the songwriters (as well as the producers) of these upcoming shows were hoping to avoid the debacle of 1990's quickly closing *Shogun*, a Broadway fate regarded as something near inevitable for all but Andrew Lloyd Webber, but even Lloyd Webber's *Aspects of Love* wilted early under the dim Broadway bulbs this year.

The odds did not deter Lynn Ahrens and Stephen Flaherty, however. The winners of the Richard Rodgers award for their 1988 play *Lucky Stiff* were Broadway's newest darlings surviving into 1991 with the Caribbean-flavored *Once on This Island*. Off-Broadway, William Finn failed in his *Return to Falsettoland* to recreate the resonance of his earlier play, *March of the Falsettos*, while Craig Carnelia, with no book to work on, chose last year's Maltby-Shire *Closer Than Ever* route by performing tunes from his catalogue, in a revue entitled *Pictures in the Hallway*.

By far the most astonishing credits in the theatrical world of 1990 were those garnered by Stephen Sondheim for authoring three songs for Madonna in the film *Dick Tracy* ("More," "What Can You Lose," and "Sooner or Later (I Always Get My Man)," which won an Academy Award). Maybe he'd already lost his virginity when he rewrote "Putting It Together," for Barbra Streisand's *The Broadway Album* (and then let the tune be used in a Xerox commercial). Or maybe, he too, like the rest of us, had come to understand the rare potential of a movie to transform a song into a monumental event (such as when Meryl Streep took to the stage in *Postcards from the Edge* to perform Shel Silverstein's country lament "I'm Checking Out"). More probably, he was just hoping that a hit song might be lifted from the soundtrack album, as it was for other MTV-ready films, like *Young Guns II* ("Blaze of Glory"), *Pretty Woman* ("It Must Have Been Love," "King of Wishful Thinking"), and *Ghost* (whose signature standard, "Unchained Melody," by the Righteous Brothers, effectively competed with the ghost of itself, with an older version of the tune from a previous Righteous Brothers album battling the soundtrack version, as they both scaled the charts).

The Emotions of Country Music

Country songs benefitted from multimedia exposure this year as well, with the most powerful performance of the year being that by the aforementioned

Popular Music in 1990

Meryl Streep (if Roseanne Barr rates an album for twisting the National Anthem, Streep surely rates a boxed set, or at least a starring role in *The Patsy Cline Story*). A close second to Meryl would have to be Mary Chapin Carpenter's nationally televised performance, delighting the jaded, bejeweled crowd at the Country Music Awards with the caustic "Opening Act." An opening act no longer, Mary later achieved headliner status with "You Win Again."

The Grammy for Country Song of the Year, however, went to Don Henry and Jon Vezner, for their tearjerker, "Where've You Been" (an almost certain bet to be made into a future TV movie of the week), emotionally rendered by Kathy Mattea, who gained added, if perhaps unfair, insight into the very personal lyrics by virtue of being married to co-author Vezner. Elsewhere in that very traditional bastion, Paul Overstreet continued to mine familiar familial territory in "Seein' My Father in Me," while the sorely taxed Willie Nelson sought his traditional escape in "The Highway" and Garth Brooks found escape of another kind among the dregs in "Friends in Low Places." When it comes to love and loss, no other type of music comes close to touching the messy essence of existence like country music, this year epitomized by Hugh Prestwood's "Hard Rock Bottom of Your Heart," a hit for Randy Travis, but hardly a household tune.

Now, if only Bette Midler could get a hold of it.

A

Absolutely Swing
Words and music by Gerome Ragni, James Rado, and Galt
  MacDermot.
Introduced by the songwriters Gerome Ragni, James Rado and Galt
  MacDermot. From a forthcoming musical, *Sun*, their first work
  together since *Hair*.

Aces
Words and music by Cheryl Wheeler.
Cheryl Wheeler Music, 1990/Bug Music, 1990.
Introduced by Cheryl Wheeler in *Circles and Arrows* (Capitol, 90).

Acquainted with the Night
Words by Robert Frost, music by Brooks Williams.
Red Guitar Blue Music, 1989.
Introduced by Brooks Williams on *North from Statesboro* (Red Guitar
  Blue Music, 90). Adapted from the poem by Robert Frost.

Across the River
Words and music by Bruce Hornsby and John Hornsby.
Zappo Music, 1990/Basically Gasp Music, 1990/Bob-a-Lew Songs,
  1990.
Introduced by Bruce Hornsby & The Range on *A Night on the Town*
  (RCA, 90).

After the Rain
Words and music by Matt Wilson, Gunnar Nelson, Mark Tanner,
  and R. Wilson.
Matt-Black, 1990/Gunster, 1990/EMI-April Music Inc.,
  1990/Otherwise Publishing, 1990/BMG Music, 1990/Second Hand
  Songs, 1990.
Best-selling record by Nelson from *After the Rain* (DGC, 90). The
  Nelson brothers are sons of the late rocker Ricky Nelson.

Ain't Gonna Come Till I'm Ready (Irish)
Words and music by Karl Wallinger.
Polygram International, 1990.
Introduced by World Party on *Goodbye Jumbo* (Chrysalis, 90). Irish
singer-songwriter is former member of the Waterboys.

Air
Words by Frank O'Hara, music by Ricky Ian Gordon.
Introduced by Angelina Reaux in *Sweet Song*, a one-woman show.
Song based on poem by Frank O'Hara.

All Around the World (English)
Words and music by Lisa Stansfield, Ian Devaney, and Andy Morris.
BMG Music, 1989/Block & Gilbert, 1989.
Best-selling record by Lisa Stansfield from *Affection* (Arista, 90). First
single by a white artist to top the R&B charts since George
Michael's "One More Try."

All for You
Words and music by David Baerwald.
Almo Music Corp., 1990/Zen of Iniquity, 1990/Little Reata,
1990/Dee Klein, 1990.
Introduced by David Baerwald on *Bedtime Stories* (A&M, 90). Former
member of David and David.

All I Do Is Think of You
Words and music by Michael Lovesmith and Brian Holland.
Stone Diamond Music Corp., 1989/Gold Forever Music Inc., 1990.
Best-selling record by Troop from *Attitude* (Atlantic, 89).

All I Wanna Do Is Make Love to You (English)
Words and music by Robert John Lange.
Zomba Enterprises, Inc., 1979.
Best-selling record by Heart from *Brigade* (Capitol, 90). Writer Lange
is well-known rock record producer (Def Leppard).

All My Life
Best-selling record by Linda Ronstadt (featuring Aaron Neville) from
Cry Like a Rainstorm, Howl Like the Wind (Elektra, 89). For
copyright information, see *Popular Music, 1989*.

All or Nothing (East German)
English words and music by Frank Farian, Dietman Kawohl, and
Harold Baierl.
MCA Music, 1990/EMI-Blackwood Music Inc., 1990/Bay.
Best-selling record by Milli Vanilli from *Girl You Know It's True*
(Arista, 89). Fifth consecutive Top 10 single by singing group later

revealed as merely a lip-synching dance act that didn't sing on their records or in concert.

Alone in the World
Words by Alan Bergman and Marilyn Bergman, music by Jerry Goldsmith.
Threesome Music, 1990/MCA Music, 1990.
Introduced by Patti Austin in the film and on the soundtrack album *The Russia House* (MCA, 90).

Alright
Words and music by Janet Jackson, James Harris, III, and Terry Lewis.
Black Ice Music, 1989/Flyte Tyme Tunes, 1989.
Best-selling record by Janet Jackson from *Rhythm Nation 1814* (A&M, 89). Nominated for a Grammy Award for Best Rhythm 'n' Blues Song of the Year.

Another Day in Paradise (English)
For copyright information see *Popular Music 1989*. Phil Collins' best-selling 1989 record won him a Grammy Award, Record of the Year, 1990. Nominated for Grammy Award, Song of the Year, 1990.

Answer Me (Scottish)
Words and music by Jimmie O'Neill.
Introduced by The Silencers on *A Blues for Buddah* (RCA, 89).

Anything But Lonely (English)
Music by Andrew Lloyd Webber, words by Charles Hart and Don Black.
Really Useful Group, 1989.
Introduced by Ann Crumb in the musical *Aspects of Love* (90).

Armed with a Broken Heart
Words and music by John Gorka.
Blues Palace, 1990.
Introduced by John Gorka on *Land of the Bottom Line* (Windham Hill, 90). New voice on the folk scene.

Arrest in Effect
Words and music by Luther Campbell and The 2 Live Crew.
Pac Jam Publishing, 1990.
Introduced by Luke, Featuring The 2 Live Crew on *Banned in the U.S.A.* (Atlantic, 90). Detailing their trials and tribulations as rap's most troubling cause celebre.

Ashokan Farewell
Music by Jay Ungar.
Sleeping Bag Music, 1983.
Revived by Fiddle Fever on the PBS Series *The Civil War* and on the
soundtrack *The Civil War* (Elektra, Nonesuch 90). Originally
recorded on *Waltz of the Wind* (Flying Fish).

B

Baby, It's Tonight
Words and music by Jude Cole.
Coleision, 1990/EMI-Blackwood Music Inc., 1990.
Best-selling record by Jude Cole from *A View from 3rd Street* (Reprise, 90).

Back in My Younger Days
Words and music by Danny Flowers.
Danny Flowers, 1990/Bug Music, 1990.
Best-selling record by Don Williams from *True Love* (RCA, 90).

Banned in the U.S.A.
Words and music by Bruce Springsteen and Featuring The 2 Live Crew Luke.
Bruce Springsteen Publishing, 1984.
Best-selling record by Luke featuring The 2 Live Crew from *Banned in the U.S.A.* (Atlantic, 90). Borrowing Bruce Springsteen's anti-war anthem for their own self-defensive purposes.

B.B.D. (I Thought It Was Me)
Words and music by Roney Hooks, Eric Sadler, Keith Shocklee, D. Durant, and P. Stewart.
Ronestone, 1990/AlshaMighty/Nia, 1990/Your Mother's/Strong Island, 1990.
Best-selling record by Bell Biv Devoe from *Poison* (MCA, 90). Bell, Biv and Devoe are former members of New Edition.

Beautiful Red Dress
Words and music by Laurie Anderson.
Difficult Music, 1989.
Introduced by Laurie Anderson in *Strange Angels* (Warner Bros, 90). A return of the noted performance artist.

Because I Love You (The Postman Song)
Words and music by W. Allen Brooks.
Saja Music, 1990/Mya-T, 1990.
Best-selling record by Stevie B from *Love & Emotion* (LMR, 90).

Ben Turpin in the Army
Words and music by Joseph Lee Henry.
True North Music, 1990/Almo Music Corp.
Introduced by Joe Henry on *Shuffletown* (A&M, 90).

Better Not Tell Her
Words and music by Carly Simon.
C'est Music, 1990.
Introduced by Carly Simon in *Have You Seen Me Lately* (Arista, 90).

Big Beautiful Planet (Canadian)
Words and music by Raffi.
Homeland, 1982.
Introduced by Raffi on *Evergreen* (MCA, 90). An environmental ode
by the children's singer.

Big Blue Wonder
Words and music by Brooks Williams.
Red Guitar Blue Music, 1989.
Introduced by Brooks Williams on *North from Statesboro* (Red Guitar
Blue Music, 90).

Big Northern Lights (English)
Words and music by Martin George Stephenson.
Kitchen Music, 1990/EMI Songs Ltd./EMI-Blackwood Music Inc.
Introduced by Martin Stephenson & The Daintees on *Salutation Road*
(Capitol, 90).

Big World
Words and music by Bill Bonk and Phil Parlapiano.
Figaro Music, 1990.
Introduced by The Brothers Figaro on *Gypsy Beat* (Geffen, 90).

Bigger Picture (Scottish)
Words and music by Mike Scott.
Copyright Control, 1990.
Introduced by The Waterboys on *Room to Roam* (Ensign, 90).

Bird on a Wire (Canadian)
Revived by The Neville Brothers in the film *Bird on a Wire*. Also
included on their album *River of Time* (A&M, 90). For copyright
information, see *Popular Music 1920-1979*.

Birdhouse in Your Soul
Words and music by They Might Be Giants.
They Might Be Giants Music, 1989.
Introduced by They Might Be Giants on *Flood* (Elektra, 90).
Innovative cross between the Beach Boys and PDQ Bach.

Birthday (English)
Revived by Paul McCartney on *Tripping the Light Fantastic* (Capitol,
90). Live recording from 89-90 world tour. For copyright
information see *Popular Music 1920-1979.*

Black Cat
Words and music by Janet Jackson.
Black Ice Music, 1989.
Best-selling record by Janet Jackson from *Rhythm Nation 1814* (A&M,
89).

Black Dog/Hound Dog
Words and music by Jimmy Page, Robert Plant, John Paul Jones,
Jerry Leiber, and Mike Stoller.
Introduced by Dread Zeppelin on *Un-Led-Ed* (IRS, 90). Year's best
one-joke band combined an Elvis look-alike with the tunes of Led
Zeppelin. For copyright information, see *Popular Music, 1920-1979.*

Black President (South African)
Music by Fello Twala, English words by Brenda Fassie.
EMI-South Africa, Saudi Arabia, 1990.
Introduced by Brenda Fassie in *Brenda Fassie* (SBK, 90).
Anti-apartheid lyric was banned in South Africa. Story of Nelson
Mandela written and sung by his niece.

Black Velvet (Canadian)
Words and music by David Tyson and Christopher Ward.
Bluebear Waltzes, 1990/EMI-Blackwood Music Inc., 1990/David
Tyson.
Best-selling record by Alannah Myles from *Alannah Myles* (Atlantic,
90). Evoking the ghost of Presley-past.

Blaze of Glory (from *Young Guns II*)
Words and music by Jon Bon Jovi.
Bon Jovi Publishing, 1990/PRI Music, 1990.
Best-selling record by Jon Bon Jovi from the film *Young Guns II* and
its soundtrack album *Blaze of Glory* (Polygram, 90). Jon Bon Jovi in
a solo effort. Nominated for an Academy Award, Best Original
Song, 1990. Nominated for a Grammy Award, Best TV/Film Song,
1990.

The Blues
Words and music by Dwayne Wiggins and Ray Wiggins.
Tony! Toni! Tone!, 1990/PRI Music, 1990.
Best-selling record by Tony! Toni! Tone! from *The Revival* (Polydor, 90).

Blues Before and After
Words and music by Pat DiNizio.
Famous Monster, 1989/Screen Gems-EMI Music Inc., 1989.
Introduced by The Smithereens on *11* (Capitol, 89).

A Blues for Buddah (Scottish)
Words and music by Jimmie O'Neill.
Introduced by The Silencers on *A Blues for Buddah* (RCA, 89).

Born at the Right Time
Words and music by Paul Simon.
Paul Simon Music, 1989.
Introduced by Paul Simon on *The Rhythm of the Saints* (Warner Bros., 90). Simon follows up *Graceland* LP with a tribute to the music of Brazil.

Born in Chicago
Words and music by Nick Gravenites.
Warner-Tamerlane Publishing Corp., 1965.
Released by The Pixies on *Rubaiyat* (Elektra, 90). The Paul Butterfield Blues Band classic revived by alternative rockers.

Brothers
Words and music by Jimmie Vaughan and Stevie Ray Vaughan.
Stevie Ray Songs, 1990/R Mode Music/Copyright Management Icn.
Introduced by The Vaughan Brothers on *Family Style* (Epic, 90). Recorded just before plane crash claimed blues guitar great Stevie Ray.

Brothers Gonna Work It Out
Words and music by Keith Shocklee, Chuck D (pseudonym for Charles Ridenhour), and Eric Sadler.
Def American Songs, 1990/Your Mother's.
Introduced by Public Enemy on *Fear of a Black Planet* (Def Jam/Columbia, 90). Celebrated follow-up to *We're a Nation of Millions*.

The Buddy System
Music by Cy Coleman, words by David Zippel.

Notable Music Co., Inc., 1989/WB Music Corp.

Introduced by Rene Auberjanois in the musical and its cast album *City of Angels* (Columb ia, 90).

Burn Hollywood Burn

Words and music by Chuck D (pseudonym for Charles Ridenhour), Flavor Flav (pseudonym for William Drayton), and Terminator X (pseudonym for Norman Rogers).

Def American Songs, 1990/Your Mother's, 1990.

Introduced by Public Enemy on *Fear of a Black Planet* (Def Jam/Columbia, 90). Strong statements from rap's most literate spokesmen.

But Anyway

Words and music by Chan Kinchla and John Popper.

Blues Traveler, 1990/Irving Music Inc., 1990.

Introduced by The Blues Travelers on *Pave the Earth* (A&M, 90), a new music sampler.

C

Can't Stop
Words and music by L. A. Reid (pseudonym for Antonio Reid) and
  Babyface (pseudonym for Kenny Edmunds).
Hip-Trip Music Co., 1989/Kear Music.
Best-selling record by After 7 from *After 7* (Virgin, 89). Another
  amazing year from the songwriting machine of Reid & Babyface.

Can't Stop Falling into Love
Words and music by Rick Nielsen, Robin Zander, and Tom Petersson.
Screen Gems-EMI Music Inc., 1990/Consenting Adult, 1990.
Best-selling record by Cheap Trick from *Busted* (Epic, 90).

Caroline
Words and music by Johnette Napolitano.
International Velvet, 1990/Bug Music, 1990/Dead Los Angeles,
  1990/I.R.S., 1990.
Introduced by Concrete Blonde on *Bloodletting* (IRS, 90).

Carolyn
Words and music by Steve Wynn.
Poison Brisket Music, 1990.
Introduced by Steve Wynn on *Kerosene Man* (Rhino, 90).

A Certain Someone (English)
Words and music by David Gavurin and Harriet Wheeler.
Geffen Music, 1990/WB Music Corp.
Introduced by The Sundays on *Reading, Writing and Arithmetic*
  (Geffen, 90).

Cha No Yu
Words and music by Paul Chihara.
Introduced by June Angela and Joseph Forunda in *Shogun--The
  Musical* (90).

Chains
Words and music by Hal Bynum and Bud Reneau.
Silverline Music, Inc., 1988/Andite Invasion/Cross Keys Publishing Co., Inc.
Best-selling record by Patty Loveless from *Honky Tonk Angel* (MCA, 89).

Chasin' That Neon Rainbow
Words and music by Alan Jackson and Jim McBride.
EMI-April Music Inc., 1990/Seventh Son Music Inc., 1990/Mattie Ruth, 1990.
Best-selling record by Alan Jackson on *Here in the Real World* (Arista, 90).

Cherry Pie
Words and music by Jani Lane.
Virgin Songs, 1990/Dick Dragon Music, 1990.
Best-selling record by Warrant from *Cherry Pie* (Columbia, 90). With this tune, and the success of TV series *Twin Peaks,* a great year for cherry pie.

Children of the Night
Words and music by Richard Marx.
Chi-Boy, 1989.
Best-selling record by Richard Marx from *Repeat Offender* (EMI, 89). Inspired by street people of L.A.'s Sunset Strip. Proceeds from royalties donated to Children of One Night Organization, which helps runaway kids.

Cinderella's Big Score
Words and music by Sonic Youth.
Savage Conquest Music, 1990.
Introduced by Sonic Youth on *Goo* (Geffen, 90).

Civil War
Words and music by Guns N' Roses.
Guns N' Roses Music, 1990.
Introduced by Guns N' Roses at Farm Aid benefit. Included on LP *Nobody's Child--Romanian Angel Appeal* (Warner Bros., 90).

Close to You (English)
Words and music by Gary Benson, Winston Sela, and Max Elliott.
E.G. Music, Inc., 1990/W.S., 1990/Chappell & Co., Inc., 1990/Level Vibes, 1990/Colgems-EMI Music Inc., 1990/Forever.
Best-selling record by Maxi Priest from *Bonafide* (Charisma, 90).

C'mon and Get My Love
Words and music by Danny Poku and Cathy Dennis.

EMI-Blackwood Music Inc., 1989.
Best-selling record by D-Mob introducing Cathy Dennis from *A Little Bit of This, A Little Bit of That* (Polygram, 89).

Come Back to Me
Words and music by Janet Jackson, James Harris, III, and Terry Lewis.
Black Ice Music, 1989.
Best-selling record by Janet Jackson from *Rhythm Nation 1814* (A&M, 89).

Come In
Words and music by Dianne Reeves, Billy Childs, and Dianne Louie.
Wild Honey Publishing Co., 1990/Lunacy, 1990/Duncanne Hille, 1990.
Introduced by Dianne Reeves on *Never Too Far* (EMI, 90).

Come Next Monday
Words and music by Rory Bourke, K. T. Oslin, and Charlie Black.
Tri-Chappell Music Inc., 1989/Chappell & Co., Inc./Serenity Manor.
Best-selling record by K. T. Oslin from *This Woman* (RCA, 89). Nominated for a Grammy Award for Best Country Song of the Year.

Comfortably Numb (English)
Words and music by Roger Waters and David Gilmour.
Pink Floyd, London, England, 1980.
Revived by Van Morrison on *The Wall* (Polygram, 90). From a concert celebrating the razing of the Berlin Wall. Introduced by Pink Floyd on the original album entitled *The Wall*.

Commercial Rain (English)
Words and music by Inspiral Carpets.
Chrysalis Music Corp., 1989.
Introduced by Inspiral Carpets on *Life* (Elektra, 90). The neo-psychedelic Manchester sound.

Commodore Peter
Words and music by Walter Salas-Humera.
Voltone, 1989/Music Corp. of America.
Introduced by The Silos on *The Silos* (RCA, 90). Updated roots rock.

Conspiracy of the Heart
Words and music by Steve Wynn and Johnette Napolitano.
Poison Brisket Music, 1990/Bug Music/International Velvet.
Introduced by Steve Wynn on *Kerosene Man* (Rhino, 90). Co-writer Napolitano is member of Concrete Blonde.

Cool Dry Place
Words and music by Traveling Wilburys.
Ganga Publishing Co., 1990/Zero Productions, 1990/Special Rider
  Music, 1990/EMI-April Music Inc., 1990/Gone Gator Music, 1990.
Introduced by Traveling Wilburys on *The Traveling Wilburys, Vol. 3*
  (Warner Bros., 90). Group is made up of Bob Dylan, George
  Harrison, Tom Petty and Jeff Lynne.

Cordoba (English)
Words and music by Brian Eno and John Cale.
Upala, 1990/Hamstein Music, 1990/John Cale, 1990.
Introduced by Eno/Cale on *Wrong Way Up* (Warner Bros., 90).

Could This Be Love
Words and music by Rob Clivilles.
Robi-Roy, 1989/Virgin Music, Inc., 1989.
Best-selling record by Seduction from *Nothing Matters Without Love*
  (A&M, 89).

Cradle of Love (from *Ford Fairlane*)
Words and music by David Werner and Billy Idol.
TCF, 1990/David Werner, 1990/EMI-April Music Inc.,
  1990/Boneidol Music, 1990/Chrysalis Music Corp., 1990.
Best-selling record by Billy Idol from *Charmed Life* (Chrysalis, 90) and
  from the film and soundtrack album *Ford Fairlane*.

Crazy
Words and music by Hakeem Abdulsamad and Khiry Abdulsamad.
Buff Man, 1990.
Best-selling record by The Boys from *The Boys* (Motown, 90).

Crazy in Love
Words and music by Even Stevens and Randy McCormick.
Screen Gems-EMI Music Inc., 1990.
Best-selling record by Conway Twitty on *Crazy in Love* (MCA, 90).

Cuts Both Ways
Words and music by Gloria Estefan.
Foreign Imported, 1989.
Best-selling record by Gloria Estefan from *Cuts Both Ways* (Epic, 89).

D

Dance
Words and music by David Baerwald.
Almo Music Corp., 1990/Zen of Iniquity, 1990/Little Reata,
   1990/Dee Klein, 1990.
Introduced by David Baerwald in *Bedtime Stories* (A&M, 90).

The Dance
Words and music by Tony Arata.
Morganactive Music, 1989/Pookie Bear.
Best-selling record by Garth Brooks from *Garth Brooks* (Capitol, 89).
   Nominated for a Grammy Award for Best Country Song of the
   Year.

Dangerous (Swedish)
English words and music by Per Gessle.
Jimmie Fun, Sweden, 1989.
Best-selling record by Roxette from *Look Sharp* (EMI, 89).

Days That Used to Be
Words and music by Neil Young.
Silver Fiddle, 1990.
Introduced by Neil Young & Crazy Horse on *Ragged Glory* (Reprise,
   90). A fond remembrance of trips past.

Deep Deep Trouble
Words and music by Matt Groening and DJ Jazzy Jeff.
Fox Film Music Corp., 1990/Gracie Films, 1990/Yuck
   Music/TCF/Zomba Enterprises, Inc.
Introduced by Bart Simpson on *The Simpsons Sing the Blues* (Geffen,
   90). This tune was co-written by the cartoonist who created the hit
   series.

Dig That Crazy Beat
Words and music by Wendy Wall.
EMI-Blackwood Music Inc., 1989/Waterwind.
Introduced by Wendy Wall from *Wendy Wall* (SBK, 90).

Do Me!
Words and music by Carl Bourelly, Michael Bivens, Ronnie Devoe,
    and Ricky Bell.
Willesden Music, Inc., 1990/Low Key, 1990/Baledat, 1990/Slik Star,
    1990/Unicity Music, Inc., 1990.
Best-selling record by Bell Biv Devoe from *Poison* (MCA, 90).

Do You Remember? (English)
Words and music by Phil Collins.
Phil Collins, England, 1989/Hit & Run Music/Hidden Pun.
Best-selling record by Phil Collins from *...But Seriously* (Atlantic, 89).

Don Henley Must Die
Words and music by Mojo Nixon.
Muffin Stuffin, 1990/La Rana, 1990.
Introduced by Mojo Nixon on *Otis* (Enigma, 90). The author
    previously skewered Elvis Presley and Debbie Gibson in separate
    songs.

Donkey Doctor (English)
Music by 808 State.
Perfect Songs-England, People's Republic of China, 1989/ZTT
    Records Ltd.
Introduced by 808 State on *Ninety* (Tommy Boy, 90). Also found on
    the sampler *Artist Breaker*.

Don't Ask My Neighbors
Words and music by Skip Scarborough.
Warner/Unichappell, 1977.
Revived by Nancy Wilson on *Lady with a Song* (Columbia, 90).
    Introduced by The Emotions, who sing back-up on this tune.

Don't Give Us a Reason
Words and music by Hank Williams, Jr.
Bocephus Music Inc., 1990.
Introduced by Hank Williams, Jr. on *America, The Way I See It*
    (Warner/Curb, 90). Relating to activities in the Persian Gulf.

Don't Go Away Mad (Just Go Away)
Words and music by Nikki Sixx and Mick Mars.
Motley Crue, 1989/Sikki Nixx/Mick Mars.
Best-selling record by Motley Crue from *Dr. Feelgood* (Elektra, 89).

Don't Wanna Fall in Love (Canadian)
Words and music by Jane Child.
Radical Dichotomy, 1990.
Best-selling record by Jane Child from *Jane Child* (Warner Bros, 90).

Doubleback
Words and music by Billy Gibbons, Dusty Hill, and Frank Beard.
Hamstein Music, 1990/MCA Music.
Best-selling record by ZZ Top from the film *Back to the Future Part III*. The instrumental is found on the film's soundtrack (Warner Bros., 90), while the hit single is found on the group's *Recycler* (90) LP.

Down All the Days (to 1992) (English)
Words and music by Ray Davies.
Davray Music, Ltd., London, England, 1990.
Introduced by The Kinks as the unofficial anthem for the unification of the European Common Market.

The Downeaster 'Alexa'
Words and music by Billy Joel.
Joel, 1989.
Introduced by Billy Joel in *Storm Front* (Columbia, 89). Tale of embattled fishermen on Long Island.

A Dream
Words and music by Lou Reed and John Cale.
Metal Machine Music, 1989/John Cale.
Introduced by Lou Reed and John Cale on *Songs for Drella* (Sire, 90). Former members of Velvet Underground in a haunting tribute/eulogy to their former mentor, Andy Warhol.

Drunken Hearted Man
Words and music by Robert Johnson.
King of Spades Music, 1990.
Released by Robert Johnson on *The Complete Recordings* (Columbia, 90). Newly collected and mastered rare tracks from the legendary bluesman.

Dumas Walker
Words and music by Kentucky Headhunters.
Three Headed, 1989/PRI Music/Head Cheese/PRI Songs.
Best-selling record by Kentucky Headhunters from *Pickin' on Nashville* (Polygram, 90)

E

Ellie My Love (Japanese)
Japanese words and music by Keisuke Kutawa, English words and
music by Rumiko Wernes.
Burning Publishing Co. Ltd., 1979/Fuju Pacific Music, Inc.
Revived by Ray Charles on *Would You Believe?* Introduced by
Southern All Stars (79). Song is also a commercial for Suntory White
Whiskey. Charles' tune went Top 10 in Japan, before being included
on LP.

Elvis Is Dead
Words and music by Vernon Reid.
Famous Music Corp., 1990/Dare to Dream Music, 1990.
Introduced by Living Colour on *Time's Up* (Epic, 90).

The Emergence of Political Thought 1960-1990
Words and music by Andrew Ratsin.
Liu Tunes, 1989.
Introduced by Electric Bonsai Band on *I Am Joe's Eyes* (Yellow Tail,
90). Actually an acoustic solo effort by Andrew Ratsin, formerly of
Uncle Bonsai.

Emperor's New Clothes (Irish)
Words and music by Sinead O'Connor.
EMI Music Publishing, Ltd., London, England, 1990/Promostraat,
1990.
Best-selling record by Sinead O'Connor from *I Do Not Want What I
Haven't Got* (Ensign/Chrysalis, 90).

Enjoy the Silence (English)
Words and music by Martin Gore.
Emile Music, 1990.
Best-selling record by Depeche Mode from *Violator* (Sire, 90).

Epic
Words and music by Faith No More.
Big Thrilling Music, 1989/Vomit God, 1989.
Best-selling record by Faith No More from *The Real Thing* (Slash/Reprise, 90).

Escapade
Words and music by James Harris, III, Terry Lewis, and Janet Jackson.
Black Ice Music, 1989/Flyte Tyme Tunes.
Best-selling record by Janet Jackson from *Rhythm Nation 1814* (A&M, 89). Along with Prince and Michael Jackson, third artist ever to have two number one hits on R&B, dance and Top 100 charts.

Esmeralda's Hollywood
Words and music by Steve Earle and Maria McKee.
Goldline Music Inc., 1990/Duke of Earle, 1990/Little Diva Music, 1990/WB Music Corp., 1990.
Introduced by Steve Earle and the Dukes on *The Hard Way* (MCA, 90).

Ever Since I Stole the Blues
Words and music by Mose Allison.
Audre Mae Music, 1990.
Introduced by Mose Allison on *My Backyard* (Blue Note, 90). Legendary jazz singer still cooking after all these years.

Everybody Everybody (Italian)
English words and music by Mirko Limoni, Daniele Davoli, and Valerio Semplici.
Lambardoni Edizioni, 1990/Intersong, USA Inc., 1990.
Best-selling record by Black Box from *Dreamland* (RCA, 90). Lead vocal by ex-Weather Girl Martha Wash, who had to sue to get credit.

Eyes on the Prize
Words and music by Dianne Reeves and George Duke.
Wild Honey Publishing Co., 1989/Mycenae Music Publishing Co.
Introduced by Dianne Reeves on *Never Too Far* (Blue Note, 90). Duke is Reeves' cousin. Song dedicated to her grandmother.

F

A Face in the Crowd
Words and music by Tom Petty and Jeff Lynne.
Gone Gator Music, 1989/EMI-April Music Inc.
Introduced by Tom Petty on *Full Moon Fever* (MCA, 89).

Faces and Names
Words and music by Lou Reed and John Cale.
Metal Machine Music, 1989/John Cale.
Introduced by Lou Reed and John Cale on *Songs for Drella* (Sire, 90).

Falling
Music by Angelo Badalamenti, words by David Lynch.
Anlon Music Co./O.K. Paul Music.
Introduced by Julee Cruise on *Floating into the Night* (Warner Bros,
  90). Used in the TV show & soundtrack LP *Twin Peaks* (Warner
  Bros., 90).

Far from Home
Words and music by Monica Walker, Nathan Wang, and Geno
  Escarrega.
Warner-Tamerlane Publishing Corp., 1990.
Introduced by Dana Delany in TV series and soundtrack LP *China
  Beach--Music and Memories* (SBK, 90).

Fear of a Black Planet
Words and music by Chuck D (pseudonym for Charles Ridenhour).
Def American Songs, 1990/Your Mother's, 1990.
Introduced by Public Enemy in *Fear of a Black Planet* (Def
  Jam/Columbia, 90).

Feels Good
Words and music by Dwayne Wiggins, Ray Wiggins, Timothy
  Christian, and Caron Wheeler.

Tony! Toni! Tone!, 1990/PRI Music, 1990.
Best-selling record by Tony! Toni! Tone! from *The Revival* (Polydor, 90).

A Few Ole Country Boys
Words and music by Troy Seals and Mentor Williams.
WB Music Corp., 1990/Two-Sons Music, 1990/Bamatuck, 1990/Mentor Williams, 1990.
Introduced by Randy Travis and George Jones on *Duets* (Warner Bros., 90).

57 Channels (and Nothin' On)
Words and music by Bruce Springsteen.
Bruce Springsteen Publishing, 1990.
Introduced by Bruce Springsteen at a benefit concert in Los Angeles for the Christic Institute.

Fire on the Cross
Words and music by Bruce Hornsby and John Hornsby.
Zappo Music, 1990/Basically Gasp Music, 1990/Bob-a-Lew Songs, 1990.
Introduced by Bruce Hornsby & The Range on *A Night on the Town* (RCA, 90). The South's premier scribe takes on the Ku Klux Klan.

Fires of Eden
Words and music by Kit Hain and Mark Goldenberg.
Reata Publishing Inc., 1990/Kittus Corp., 1990/Music Corp. of America, 1990/Fleedleedee Music, 1990.
Introduced by Judy Collins on *Fires of Eden* (Columbia, 90).

First Girl I Loved (English)
Words and music by Robin Williamson.
Warner-Tamerlane Publishing Corp., 1967.
Revived by Jackson Browne on *Rubaiyat* (Elektra, 90). Originated by the Incredible String Band.

The First Time
Words and music by Bernard Jackson and Brian Simpson.
Colgems-EMI Music Inc., 1990/Stansbury, 1990.
Best-selling record by Surface from *3 Deep* (Columbia, 90).

Five Minutes
Words and music by Beth Nielsen Chapman.
BMG Music, 1985.
Best-selling record by Lorrie Morgan from *Leave the Light On* (RCA, 89).

Fly to the Angels
Words and music by Mark Slaughter and Dana Strum.
Topless, 1990/Chrysalis Music Corp.
Best-selling record by Slaughter from *Stick It to Ya* (Chrysalis, 90).

Forever
Words and music by Paul Stanley and Michael Bolton.
Stanley World, 1989/Hori Productions America Inc./Mr. Bolton's
  Music/Warner-Tamerlane Publishing Corp.
Best-selling record by Kiss from *Hot in the Shade* (Mercury, 89).

Forever Changed
Words and music by Lou Reed and John Cale.
Metal Machine Music, 1989/John Cale.
Introduced by Lou Reed and John Cale on *Songs for Drella* (Sire, 90).

Forever Yours
Words by Lynn Ahrens, music by Stephen Flaherty.
WB Music Corp., 1990/Warner-Tamerlane Publishing
  Corp./Hillsdale Music/Stephen Flaherty.
Introduced by La Chanze, Jerry Dixon and Eric Riley in the musical
  and original cast album of *Once on This Island* (RCA, 90).

Freedom (English)
Words and music by George Michael.
Morrison Leahy, England, 1990/Chappell & Co., Inc.
Best-selling record by George Michael from *Listen Without Prejudice,
  Vol. 1* (Columbia, 90).

Freedom of Speech
Music by Ice-T, words by Jello Biafra.
Maim That Tune, 1987/Colgems-EMI Music Inc./Rhyme Syndicate.
Revived by Ice-T on *2 Nasty for Radio* (Cold Chillin' Records, 90).
  Originated on *The Iceberg/Freedom of Speech...Just Watch What
  You Say* (Sire/WB Records). One of the year's biggest concerns was
  censorship.

Friends in Low Places
Words and music by DeWayne Blackwell and Bud Lee.
Careers Music Inc., 1990/Music Ridge.
Best-selling record by Garth Brooks from *Garth Brooks* (Capitol, 89).
  Nominated for a Grammy Award for Best Country Song of the
  Year.

From a Distance
Revived by Bette Midler on *Some People's Lives* (Atlantic, 90). For
  copyright information see *Popular Music, 1987*. Anti-war lament was

especially appropriate this year. Won a Grammy Award for Song of the Year, 1990. Nominated for a Grammy Award, Record of the Year, 1990.

Full of Life
Words and music by John Gorka.
Blues Palace, 1990.
Introduced by John Gorka on *Land of the Bottom Line* (Windham Hill, 90).

Funhouse (The House We Dance In)
Words and music by Fingerprints.
Hittage, 1990/Turnout Brothers Publishing Co.
Introduced by by Kid N' Play in the film and soundtrack album from *House Party* (Motown, 90)

Further to Fly
Words and music by Paul Simon.
Paul Simon Music, 1989.
Introduced by Paul Simon on *The Rhythm of the Saints* (Warner Bros., 90).

G

Gentle Afternoon
Words and music by Bob Merrill.
Chappell & Co., Inc., 1990.
Introduced by Julie Wilson and Leigh Beery in *Hannah...1939*.

Get Away Jordan
Words and music by Mark Kibble.
Warner-Elektra-Asylum Music Inc., 1990/Winston Kae.
Introduced by Take 6 in the TV special and its soundtrack album *Do It a Cappella* (Elektra, 90).

Get Up! (Before the Night Is Over) (Belgian)
English words and music by Manuella Kamosi and Jo Bagaert.
BMC, 1989/Bogam/Colgems-EMI Music Inc.
Best-selling record by Technotronic from *Pump Up the Jam--The Album* (SBK, 89).

Ghetto Heaven (English)
Words and music by Peter Lord, Jeffrey Smith, and Sandra St. Victor.
EMI-Blackwood Music Inc., 1990/Vermal/EMI-April Music Inc./Maanami/Leo Sun.
Best-selling record by The Family Stand from *Chain* (Atlantic, 90).

A Girl Like You
Words and music by Pat DiNizio.
Famous Monster, 1989/Screen Gems-EMI Music Inc.
Introduced by The Smithereens on *11* (Capitol, 89).

Girls Nite Out
Words and music by Daryl Ross and Sheri Byers.
Beyerson, 1990/Rossaway/Island Music/Virgin Songs/Tuff Cookie.
Best-selling record by Tyler Collins from *Girls Nite Out* (RCA, 90).

Giving You the Benefit
Words and music by L. A. Reid (pseudonym for Antonio Reid) and
Babyface (pseudonym for Kenny Edmunds).
Kear Music, 1990/Epic/Solar.
Best-selling record by Pebbles from *Always* (MCA, 90).

Glory
Words and music by Derrick Jones.
Zomba Enterprises, Inc., 1990.
Introduced by D-Nice on the album *Call Me D-Nice* (Jive, 90).
Inspired by the film of the same name.

Good Times
Words and music by Sam Cooke.
ABKCO Music Inc., 1964.
Best-selling record by Dan Seals from *On Arrival* (Capitol, 90).

Groove Is in the Heart
Words and music by Deee-Lite, Herbie Hancock, and John Davis.
Delovely, 1990/Hancock Music Co./Zomba Enterprises, Inc.
Best-selling record by Deee-Lite on *World Clique* (Elektra, 90). Dance
sensations of the year.

Gulf Coast Highway
Revived by Willie Nelson and Emmylou Harris on Emmylou's album
Duets (Reprise, 90). For copyright information see *Popular Music
1989.*

H

Hanky Panky
Words and music by Madonna Ciccone and Patrick Leonard.
WB Music Corp., 1990/Bleu Disque Music/Webo Girl Music/WB
    Music Corp./No Tomato.
Best-selling record by Madonna from *I'm Breathless* (Sire, 90). Caused
    a mini-sensation for its raunchy lyrical attitude.

Hard Rock Bottom of Your Heart
Words and music by Hugh Prestwood.
Careers Music Inc., 1989.
Best-selling record by Randy Travis from *Storms of Life* (Warner
    Bros., 89).

Hard to Handle
Words and music by Otis Redding, Alvertis Isbell, and Allen Jones.
Irving Music Inc., 1968.
Revived by The Black Crowes from *Shake Your Money Maker* (Def
    American, 90).

Have You Seen Her
Revived by M.C. Hammer from *Please Hammer Don't Hurt 'Em*
    (Capitol, 90). For copyright information see *Popular Music,
    1920-1979*.

He Walked on Water
Words and music by Allen Shamblin.
Hayes Street, 1989/Almo Music Corp.
Best-selling record by Randy Travis from *No Holdin' Back* (Warner
    Bros., 89).

Heart of Destruction (Canadian)
Words and music by Ferron.

Nemesis, 1990.
Introduced by Ferron on *Phantom Center* (Chameleon, 90). Return of Canadian folk/rock legend.

Heart of Stone (English)
Words and music by Andy Hill and Pete Sinfield.
Virgin Songs, 1989/Pillarview/Chrysalis Music Corp.
Best-selling record by Cher from *Heart of Stone* (Geffen, 89).

Heart of Stone
Words and music by Carolyn Bowden, Gregg Tripp, and Elliott Wolff.
Jesse Boy, 1989/Trippland/Virgin Songs/Elliott Wolff Music.
Best-selling record by Taylor Dayne from *Can't Fight Fate* (Arista, 89).

Heart of the City (English)
Words and music by Martin George Stephenson.
EMI Songs Ltd., 1990/Kitchen Music/EMI-Blackwood Music Inc.
Introduced by Martin Stephenson & The Daintees on *Salutation Road* (Capitol, 90).

Heart of the Matter
Words and music by Don Henley, Mike Campbell, and J. D. Souther.
Cass County Music Co./Wild Gator Music/Ice Age Music.
Best-selling record by Don Henley from *The End of the Innocence* (Geffen, 89).

The Heart That You Own
Words and music by Dwight Yoakam.
Coal Dust West, 1990.
Introduced by Dwight Yoakam on *There Was a Way* (Reprise, 90).

Heartbeat
Words and music by Kenton Nix.
Sugarbiscuit, 1988.
Revived by Seduction from *Nothing Matters Without Love* (A&M, 89). Formerly a hit for Taana Gardner.

Heaven Knows
Words and music by Derek Bramble.
Virgin Songs, 1990.
Best-selling record by Lalah Hathaway from *Lalah Hathaway* (Virgin, 90).

Helena by the Avenue
Words and music by Joseph Lee Henry.
True North Music, 1990/Almo Music Corp.
Introduced by Joe Henry on *Pave the Earth* (A&M, 90). Recorded on *Shuffletown* (A&M, 90).

Hello, I Love You
Revived by The Cure on *Rubaiyat* (Elektra, 90). For copyright information see *Popular Music, 1920-1979.*

Hello It's Me
Words and music by Lou Reed and John Cale.
Metal Machine Music, 1989/John Cale.
Introduced by Lou Reed and John Cale on *Songs for Drella* (Sire, 90).

Help Me Hold On
Words and music by Travis Tritt and Pat Terry.
Tree Publishing Co., Inc., 1990/End of August, 1990/Post Oak, 1990.
Best-selling record by Travis Tritt from *Country Club* (Warner Bros., 90).

Here and Now
For copyright information see *Popular Music, 1989.* Luther Vandross' 1989 hit was nominated for a Grammy Award, Best Rhythm 'n' Blues Song of the Year, 1990.

Here in the Real World
Words and music by Alan Jackson and Mattie Irwin.
Mattie Ruth, 1989/Seventh Son Music Inc., 1989/Ten Ten Tunes, 1989.
Best-selling record by Alan Jackson from *Here in the Real World* (Arista, 89).

Here We Are
Words and music by Gloria Estefan.
Foreign Imported, 1989.
Best-selling record by Gloria Estefan from *Cuts Both Ways* (Epic, 89).

Here's Where the Story Ends (English)
Words and music by David Gavurin and Harriet Wheeler.
Geffen Music, 1990/WB Music Corp., 1990.
Introduced by The Sundays on *Reading, Writing and Arithmetic* (DGC, 90).

High Enough
Words and music by Tommy Shaw, Ted Nugent, and Jack Blades.
Ranch Rock, 1990/Warner-Tamerlane Publishing Corp., 1990/Tranquility Base Songs, 1990/WB Music Corp., 1990/Broadhead, 1990.
Best-selling record by Damn Yankees from *Damn Yankees* (Warner Bros., 90). Made up of former members of Styx, Night Ranger, and the original wild man of jungle rock, Ted Nugent.

The Highway
Words and music by Tom Conners and Richard Wesley.
J.D. Sandefer, 1985.
Introduced by Willie Nelson on *The Highwaymen 2* (Columbia, 90).

Highway of Dreams (Canadian)
Words and music by Jeff Healey and Joe Rockman.
See the Light, 1990.
Introduced by The Jeff Healey Band on *Hell to Pay* (Arista, 90).

Hippychick (English)
Words and music by Tim Brinkhurst.
Polygram International, 1990.
Best-selling record by Soho from *Goddess* (Atco, 90).

Hold On
Words and music by Chynna Phillips, Glen Ballard, and Carnie
Wilson.
Wilphill, 1989/EMI-Blackwood Music Inc./MCA Music/Aerostation
Corp.
Best-selling record by Wilson Phillips from *Wilson Phillips* (SBK, 90).
Nominated for a Grammy Award for Best Song of the Year.

Hold On (English)
Words and music by Thom McElroy, Denzil Foster, and En Vogue.
Two Tuff-Enuff Publishing, 1990.
Best-selling record by En Vogue from *Born to Sing* (Atlantic, 90).

Holdin' a Good Hand
Words and music by Rob Crosby and Johnny Few.
Songs of Grand Coalition Malaco Music, 1990/Marledge, 1990.
Best-selling record by Lee Greenwood. Introduced by Jimmy Williams
(Gallery, 90). Also recorded by Debbie Sigman (ESU, 90).

Hollywood Squares
Words and music by Wayland Patton, Larry Cordle, and Jeff
Tanguay.
Polygram International, 1988/Monsari, 1988/Amanda-Lin.
Introduced by George Strait on *Beyond the Blue Neon* (MCA, 89).

Home
Words and music by Andrew Spooner and William Lehner.
Texas Wedge, 1990.
Best-selling record by Joe Diffie from *A Thousand Winding Roads*
(Epic, 90).

How 'Bout Us
Revived by Grayson Hugh and Betty Wright in film and soundtrack album *True Love* (RCA, 90). Was a hit by Champaign in 1981. For copyright information, see *Popular Music 1980-1984*.

How Can We Be Lovers
Words and music by Michael Bolton, Diane Warren, and Desmond Child.
Mr. Bolton's Music, 1989/Realsongs, 1989/Desmobile Music Co., 1989/EMI-April Music Inc., 1989/Warner-Chappell Music, 1989.
Best-selling record by Michael Bolton from *Soul Provider* (Columbia, 89).

The Human Heart
Words by Lynn Ahrens, music by Stephen Flaherty.
WB Music Corp., 1990/Warner-Tamerlane Publishing Corp., 1990/Hillsdale Music, 1990/Stephen Flaherty, 1990.
Introduced by Andrea Frierson & Company in the musical and original cast album of *Once on This Island* (RCA, 90).

The Humpty Dance (English)
Words and music by Greg Jacobs and Edward Humphries.
GLG Two, 1990/Pubhowyalike, 1990.
Best-selling record by Digital Underground from *Sex Packets* (Tommy Boy, 90). Epitomizing the new disco craze.

I

I Am the Storm
Words and music by Cliff Eberhardt.
Aixoise Music, 1990/Eberhardt Music, 1990.
Introduced by Cliff Eberhardt on *The Long Road* (Windham Hill, 90).

I Believe
Words and music by Lou Reed and John Cale.
Metal Machine Music, 1989/John Cale, 1990.
Introduced by Lou Reed and John Cale in *Songs for Drella* (Sire, 90).

I Can't Understand
Words and music by Cesar Rosas and Willie Dixon.
Ceros, 1990/Hoochie Coochie, 1990/Bug Music, 1990.
Introduced by Los Lobos on *The Neighborhood* (Slash/Warner Bros.,
   90). Blues great Dixon is a collaborator on this track.

I Don't Have the Heart
Words and music by Allen Rich and Judd Friedman.
Music Corp. of America, 1990/Nelana Music, 1990/MCA Music,
   1990/Music by Candlelight/PSO Ltd., 1990.
Best-selling record by James Ingram from *It's Real* (Warner Bros., 90).
   One of the year's biggest ballads.

I Dreamed I Saw Phil Ochs Last Night (English)
Words by Billy Bragg, music by Earl Robinson.
MCA Music, 1938, 1990/Chappell & Co., Inc., 1990.
Introduced by Billy Bragg on *The Internationale* (Elektra/Utility, 90).
   Updating both the old Union anthem "Joe Hill" and its Phil Ochs
   revival "I Dreamed I Saw Joe Hill."

I Eat Dinner (Canadian)
Words and music by Kate McGarrigle.

Garden Court Music Co., 1990.
Introduced by Kate & Anna McGarrigle in *Heartbeats Accelerating* (Private, 90). Folk singing sisters in a fine comeback effort.

I Enjoy Being a Girl
Revived by Roseanne Barr on *I Enjoy Being a Girl* (Hollywood Records, 90). Satirical masterstroke by the comedy diva. For copyright information see *Popular Music, 1920-1979*.

I Fell in Love
Words and music by Carlene Carter, Howie Epstein, Benmont Tench, and Perry Lamek.
EMI Music Publishing, Ltd., London, England, 1990/Chrysalis Music Corp., 1990/Blue Gator Music, 1990/Colgems-EMI Music Inc., 1990/Carlooney Tunes, 1990/He Dog, 1990/Doraflo, 1990/Lamek Pub., 1990/Laughing Dogs, 1990/Twyla Dent Music, 1990.
Best-selling record by Carlene Carter from *I Fell in Love* (Reprise, 90).

I Found Out (English)
Words and music by Hugh Priestman.
Virgin Songs, 1990/Priestman, 1990.
Introduced by The Christians on *Colour* (Island, 90).

I Go to Extremes
Words and music by Billy Joel.
Joel, 1989.
Best-selling record by Billy Joel from *Storm Front* (Columbia, 89).

I Got Your Number
Words and music by Fred Koller, John Hiatt, and Al Anderson.
Lucrative, 1990/Lillybilly, 1990/Tomata du Plenti, 1990.
Introduced by Fred Koller on *Where the Fast Lane Ends* (Alcazar, 90).

I Left My Wallet in El Segundo
Words and music by A Tribe Called Quest.
Zomba Enterprises, Inc., 1990/We'll Do You, 1990.
Introduced by A Tribe Called Quest on *People's Instinctive Travels and the Paths of Rhythm* (Jive, 90). Critically acclaimed rap group brought form to new level.

I Look Good
Words and music by Bernadette Cooper.
Portrait, 1990/Epic/Solar, 1990/Slap Me One Music, 1990/Tree Publishing Co., Inc., 1990.
Introduced by Bernadette Cooper on *Drama According to Bernadette Cooper* (MCA, 90).

I Love to See You Smile
Revived by Randy Newman as the theme song for the TV Series
Parenthood. It was originally the theme for the movie on which the
series is based. For copyright information see *Popular Music, 1989.*

I Love U
Words and music by Mervyn Warren.
Warner-Elektra-Asylum Music Inc., 1990/Winston Kae,
1990/Mervyn Warren, 1990.
Introduced by Take 6 in *So Much 2 Say* (Reprise, 90).

I Meant Every Word He Said
Words and music by Curly Putman, Bucky Jones, and Joe Chambers.
Tree Publishing Co., Inc., 1987/Cross Keys Publishing Co., Inc./Joe
Chambers.
Best-selling record by Ricky Van Shelton from *RVS III* (Columbia,
90).

I Remember You
Words and music by Rachel Bolan and Dave Sabo.
New Jersey Underground, 1989.
Best-selling record by Skid Row from *Skid Row* (Atlantic, 89).

I Wanna Be Rich
Words and music by Reggie Calloway, Vince Calloway, Melvin
Gentry, and Belinda Lipscomb.
Epic/Solar, 1990/Calloco, 1990/Screen Gems-EMI Music Inc.,
1990/Jig-a-Watt Jams, 1990.
Best-selling record by Calloway from *All the Way* (Epic, 90).

I Want a Cure
Words and music by Rosanne Cash.
Chelcait Music, 1989/Bug Music, 1989.
Introduced by Rosanne Cash on *Interiors* (Columbia, 90).

I Wish It Would Rain Down (English)
Words and music by Phil Collins.
Phil Collins, England/Hit & Run Music, 1989.
Best-selling record by Phil Collins from *...But Seriously* (Atlantic, 89).
Guitar solo by Eric Clapton.

I Wouldn't Go Back
Words by Richard Maltby, Jr., music by David Shire.
Fiddleback Music Publishing Co., Inc., 1982/Progeny
Music/Revelation Music Publishing Corp./Long Pond Music.
Revived by Patrick Brady on the original cast album of *Closer Than
Ever* (RCA, 90). Introduced in the musical *Baby*, but dropped from
the show.

Ice Ice Baby (American-English)
Words and music by Vanilla Ice (pseudonym for Robbie Van
    Winkle), Earthquake, David Bowie, and Queen.
Ice Baby, 1990/QPM/Queen Music Ltd./Jones Music Co.
Best-selling record by Vanilla Ice from *To the Extreme* (SBK, 90).
    Borrowing heavily from the Queen/David Bowie hit, "Under
    Pressure."

If I Had Possession over Judgment Day
Words and music by Robert Johnson.
King of Spades Music, 1990, 1936.
Performed by Robert Johnson on *The Complete Recordings* (Columbia,
    90).

If Wishes Came True
Words and music by Russell Desalvo, Deena Charles, and Bob Steele.
Colgems-EMI Music Inc., 1990/Magnetic Force, 1990/Sun
    Face/Deena Charles/Another Stronger Song.
Best-selling record by Sweet Sensation from *Love Child* (Atco, 90).

I'll Be Good to You
Revived by Quincy Jones, featuring Ray Charles and Chaka Khan
    from *Back on the Block* (Warner, 89). Nominated for a Grammy
    Award for Best Rhythm & Blues Song of the Year. Originally a hit
    for The Brothers Johnson. For copyright information, see *Popular
    Music 1920-1979*.

I'll Be Your Everything
Words and music by Jordan Knight, Donnie Wood, and Tommy Page.
New Kids, 1990/Warner-Tamerlane Publishing Corp., 1990/Doraflo
    Music, Inc., 1990/Page Three, 1990.
Best-selling record by Tommy Page from *Paintings in My Mind*
    (Warner Bros., 90). Co-writers are members of New Kids on the
    Block, with whom Page toured.

I'll Be Your Shelter
Words and music by Diane Warren.
Realsongs, 1989.
Best-selling record by Taylor Dayne from *Can't Fight Fate* (Arista, 89).

I'll Sail This Ship Alone (English)
Words and music by Paul Heaton and David Rotheray.
Go! Discs Ltd., England, 1989.
Introduced by The Beautiful South on *Welcome to the Beautiful South*
    (Elektra, 90). Composed of former members of the Housemartins.

I'll See You in My Dreams
Words and music by Alan Pasqua and Mark Spiro.
Itsall, 1989/Irving Music Inc./Screen Gems-EMI Music Inc./Mark
  Spiro, 1989.
Best-selling record by Giant from *Last of the Runaways* (A&M, 89).

I'll Walk Every Step of the Way
Words and music by Mike Craver and Mark Hardwick.
Sapsucker, 1989/Lake of the Pine.
Introduced by the cast of *Smoke on the Mountain* at the Lambs
  Theater in New York City (90).

I'm Checking Out
Words and music by Shel Silverstein.
Evil Eye Music Inc., 1990.
Introduced by Meryl Streep in the film *Postcards from the Edge*.
  Nominated for an Academy Award, Best Original Song, 1990.

I'm Gonna Be Somebody
Words and music by Stewart Harris and Jill Colucci.
CRGI, 1990/Edisto Sound Int'l, 1990/Golden Torch Music Corp.,
  1990/Heart Street, 1990.
Best-selling record by Travis Tritt from *Country Club* (Warner Bros.,
  90).

I'm Over You
Words and music by Tim Nichols and Zack Turner.
Hannah's Eyes, 1989/Coburn, 1989.
Best-selling record by Keith Whitley from *I Wonder Do You Think of
  Me* (RCA, 89).

I'm Your Baby Tonight
Words and music by L. A. Reid (pseudonym for Antonio Reid) and
  Babyface (pseudonym for Kenny Edmunds).
Kear Music, 1990/Epic/Solar, 1990.
Best-selling record by Whitney Houston from *I'm Your Baby Tonight*
  (Arista, 90).

Images
Words and music by Lou Reed and John Cale.
Metal Machine Music, 1989/John Cale, 1989.
Introduced by Lou Reed and John Cale on *Songs for Drella* (Sire, 90).

Impulsive
Words and music by Steve Kipner and Cliff Magness.

EMI-April Music Inc., 1989/Stephen A. Kipner Music, 1989/WB
  Music Corp., 1989/Magnified, 1989.
Best-selling record by Wilson Phillips from *Wilson Phillips* (SBK, 90).

Innocent
Words and music by Robert Brookins and Bucky Jones.
Whole Nine Yards, 1990/Itself and Macdaddi, 1990/Tabraylah,
  1990/Haynestorm Music, 1990/Les Etoiles de la Musique,
  1990/Must Be Marvelous.
Best-selling record by Whispers from *More of the Night* (Capitol, 90).

Inside Out
Words and music by Traveling Wilburys.
Ganga Publishing Co., 1990/Zero Productions, 1990/Special Rider
  Music, 1990/EMI-April Music Inc., 1990/Gone Gator Music, 1990.
Introduced by The Traveling Wilburys on *The Traveling Wilburys, Vol.
  3* (Warner Bros., 90).

Institution Green
Words and music by Suzanne Vega.
AGF Music Ltd., 1990/Waifersongs Ltd.
Introduced by Suzanne Vega on *Days of Open Hand* (A&M, 90).

Into the Night
Music by Angelo Badalamenti, words by David Lynch.
Anlon Music Co., 1990/O.K. Paul Music.
Introduced by Julee Cruise in *Floating into the Night* (Warner Bros.,
  90). Used in the TV series and the soundtrack album *Twin Peaks*
  (Warner Bros., 90).

It Ain't Nothin'
Words and music by Tony Haselden.
Millhouse, 1989.
Best-selling record Keith Whitley from *I Wonder Do You Think of Me*
  (RCA, 89).

It Must Have Been Love (from *Pretty Woman*) (Swedish)
English words and music by Per Gessle.
Jimmie Fun, Sweden, 1989.
Best-selling record by Roxette from the film and soundtrack *Pretty
  Woman* (EMI, 90).

It Never Rains (in Southern California)
Words and music by Ray Wiggins and Timothy Christian.
Tony! Toni! Tone!, 1990/PRI Music, 1990.
Best-selling record by Tony! Toni! Tone! from *The Revival* (Wing, 90).

It Wasn't Me
Words and music by Lou Reed and John Cale.
Metal Machine Music, 1989/John Cale, 1989.
Introduced by Lou Reed and John Cale on *Songs for Drella* (Sire, 90).

Italian Girls
Words and music by John Gorka.
Blues Palace, 1990.
Introduced by John Gorka on *Land of the Bottom Line* (Windham Hill, 90).

It's Alright with Me
Words and music by Jorma Kaukonen.
Probullio Publishing, 1990/EMI-Blackwood Music Inc.
Introduced by Hot Tuna on *Pair a Dice Found* (Epic, 90). Return of the proto-hippie folk/rock/blues guitarist Kaukonen.

It's Gonna Be Alright
Words and music by Loris Holland, Jolyon Skinner, and Ruby Turner.
Zomba Enterprises, Inc., 1989.
Best-selling record by Ruby Turner from *Paradise* (Jive, 89).

It's the Going Home Together
Revived in *The Golden Apple.* For copyright information see *Popular Music, 1920-1979.*

Itsy Bitsy Teenie Weenie Yellow Polka Dot Bikini
Revived by Pink Derby (Casino, 90) and Bombalurina (Carpet/Polydor, 90). For copyright information see *Popular Music, 1920-1979.*

I've Come to Expect It from You
Words and music by Dean Dillon and Buddy Cannon.
Jesse Jo, 1990/Music Corp. of America, 1990/Buddy Cannon Music, 1990/PRI Music, 1990.
Best-selling record by George Strait on *Livin' It Up* (MCA, 90).

I've Cried My Last Tear for You
Words and music by Chris Waters and Tony King.
Cross Keys Publishing Co., Inc., 1988.
Best-selling record by Ricky Van Shelton from *RVS III* (Columbia, 90).

J

Janie's Got a Gun
Words and music by Steven Tyler and Tom Hamilton.
Swag Song Music, 1989.
Best-selling record Aerosmith from *Pump* (Geffen, 89).

Jazz Thing
Words and music by Branford Marsalis, Chris Martin, Keith Elam,
and L. E. Elie.
Stephanie, 1989.
Introduced by Gangstarr in the film *Mo' Better Blues* and on the
soundtrack album *Music from Mo' Better Blues* (Columbia, 90).
Tune is a rap detailing the history of jazz. Gangstarr is backed by
Branford Marsalis' quartet.

Jerk Out
Words and music by The Time.
Tionna Music, 1990/WB Music Corp., 1990.
Best-selling record by The Time from *Pandemonium* (Paisley Park,
90).

Jesse Don't Like It
Words and music by Loudon Wainwright.
Snowden/Hannibal, 1990.
Introduced by Loudon Wainwright (Hannibal, 90). Satiric commentary
on Jesse Helms and politics of repression.

Jukebox in My Mind
Words and music by Dave Gibson and Ronnie Rogers.
Maypop Music, 1990.
Best-selling record by Alabama from *Pass It on Down* (RCA, 90).

Just a Friend
Words and music by Mark Hall.

Biz Markie, 1989/Cold Chillin', 1989/WB Music Corp., 1989.
Best-selling record by Biz Markie from *The Biz Never Sleeps* (Warner
   Bros., 89).

Justify My Love
Words and music by Lenny Kravitz and Madonna Ciccone.
Miss Bessie Music, 1990.
Best-selling record by Madonna from *The Immaculate Collection*
   (Warner Bros., 90). Accompanied by a steamy video, this tune
   benefitted from the controversy.

K

Keep It Together
Words and music by Madonna Ciccone and Steve Bray.
WB Music Corp., 1989/Bleu Disque Music, 1989/Webo Girl
Music/WB Music Corp., 1989/Black Lion, 1989.
Best-selling record by Madonna from *Like a Prayer* (Sire, 89).

Killing Jar (English)
Words and music by Richard Thompson.
Beeswing Music, 1990.
Introduced by French Frith Kaiser Thompson on *Invisible Means*
(Windham Hill, 90).

King of Wishful Thinking (from *Pretty Woman*)
Words and music by Peter Cox, Richard Drummie, and Martin Page.
Martin Page, 1989/Zomba Enterprises, Inc., 1989.
Best-selling record by Go West from the film and soundtrack *Pretty
Woman* (EMI, 90).

Kiss the Girl
For copyright information see *Popular Music 1989*. Nominated for a
Grammy Award, Best Song for TV or Film, 1990.

Kiss This Thing Goodbye (Scottish)
Words and music by Justin Currie.
Theobalds, 1990.
Best-selling record by Del Amitri in *Waking Hours* (A&M, 90).

Knockin' Boots
Words and music by Candyman, W. Clarke, Betty Wright, E.
Hamilton, R. Wylie, and A. Hamilton.

Diabetic, 1990/Mille Miglia Musique, 1990/Windswept Pacific, 1990/Longitude Music, 1990/Stone Agate Music Corp., 1990.

Best-selling record by Candyman on *Ain't No Shame in My Game* (Epic, 90). Sampling tunes from Betty Wright and the group Rose Royce.

Kool Thing
Words and music by Sonic Youth.
Savage Conquest Music, 1990.

Introduced by Sonic Youth on *Goo* (DGC, 90). Spearheading the new Industrial White Noise movement in their first overground effort.

L

Last Time in Paris
Words and music by Chris DeGarmo and Geoff Tate.
Screen Gems-EMI Music Inc., 1990.
Introduced by Queensryche in the film and on the soundtrack album *Ford Fairlane* (Elektra, 90).

Lazy Afternoon
Revived by Ann Brown in *The Golden Apple* (90). For copyright information see *Popular Music 1920-1979.*

Let's Get It On
Revived by the band By All Means on *Beyond a Dream* (Island, 89). For copyright information see *Popular Music 1920-1979.*

Lies (English)
Words and music by Thom McElroy, Denzil Foster, Khayree Shaheed, and En Vogue.
Two Tuff-Enuff Publishing, 1990/Irving Music Inc., 1990.
Best-selling record by En Vogue from *Born to Sing* (Atlantic, 90).

Lift Every Voice and Sing
Revived by Melba Moore on *Soul Exposed* (Capitol, 90). Known as the Negro National Anthem. Moore is joined on the song by Anita Baker, Bobby Brown, Howard Hewitt, Freddie Jackson, the Reverend Jesse Jackson, and Stephanie Mills. For copyright information, see *Popular Music, 1900-1919.*

Listening to Old Voices
Words and music by John Hiatt.
Whistling Moon Traveler, 1990/Careers Music Inc., 1990.
Introduced by John Hiatt on *Stolen Moments* (A&M, 90).

A Little Bit of Rain
Words and music by Fred Neil.

Third Story Music Inc., 1965.
Revived by Ambitious Lovers on *Rubaiyat* (Elektra, 90).

Little John of God
Words and music by David Hidalgo and Louie Perez.
Davince Music, 1990/No K. O. Music, 1990/Bug Music, 1990.
Introduced by Los Lobos on *The Neighborhood* (Slash/Warner Bros., 90). Vocal by Levon Helm. Dedicated to the children of St. John of God School for Special Children, in New Jersey.

Livin' in the Light (English)
Words and music by Caron Wheeler and P. D. Hall.
EMI-Blackwood Music Inc., 1990/Motherman, 1990.
Best-selling record by Caron Wheeler from *UK Blak* (EMI, 90).

Living Without You
Music by Johnny Mandel, words by Randy Goodrum.
Marissa, 1990/California Phase Music, 1990.
Introduced by Ray Charles on *Would You Believe?* (Warner Bros., 90).

Looking for an Echo
Words and music by Richard Reicheg.
WB Music Corp., 1974.
Revived by The Persuasions in the TV special & its soundtrack album *Do It a Cappella* (Elektra, 90). This do-wop-inspired classic has been in their repertoire for years.

Lost Soul
Words and music by Bruce Hornsby.
Zappo Music, 1990/Bob-a-Lew Songs, 1990.
Introduced by Bruce Hornsby & The Range in *A Night on the Town* (RCA, 90).

Louisiana 1927
Words and music by Randy Newman.
Warner-Tamerlane Publishing Corp., 1974/Randy Newman Music.
Revived by Randy Newman in the film and on the soundtrack album *Blaze* (A&M, 90).

(Can't Live Without Your) Love and Affection
Words and music by Matt Nelson, Gunnar Nelson, and Mark Tanner.
Matt-Black, 1990/Gunster, 1990/Otherwise Publishing, 1990/BMG Music, 1990/EMI-April Music Inc., 1990.
Best-selling record by Nelson from *After The Rain* (Geffen, 90).

Love and Emotion
Words and music by W. Allen Brooks.

Saja Music, 1990/Mya-T, 1990.
Best-selling record by Stevie B from *Love & Emotion* (RCA, 90).

Love Changes Everything (English)
Music by Andrew Lloyd Webber, words by Don Black and Charles
   Hart.
Really Useful Group, 1989.
Performed by Michael Ball in the musical and on the soundtrack
   Aspects of Love (Polygram, 90).

Love Child
Revived by Sweet Sensation from *Love Child* (Atco, 90). For copyright
   information see *Popular Music 1920-1979*.

Love Is a Long Road
Words and music by Tom Petty and Mike Campbell.
Gone Gator Music, 1989/Wild Gator Music, 1989/WB Music Corp.,
   1989.
Introduced by Tom Petty on *Full Moon Fever* (MCA, 89).

Love Is Our Cross to Bear
Words and music by John Gorka.
Blues Palace, 1988.
Introduced by John Gorka on *Land of the Bottom Line* (Windham
   Hill, 90).

Love Junkie
Words by Amanda McBroom, music by Steve Geyer.
Introduced by the voice of Mara Getz in the TV series *Cop Rock*, and
   lip-synched in the show by a female mud wrestler.

Love Like This
Words and music by Pat Bunch, Pam Rose, and Mary Ann Kennedy.
Aresville, 1984/Egypt Hollow, 1984/My Choy, 1984.
Introduced by Kennedy-Rose on *hai ku* (Pangea, 89).

Love Me Down
Words and music by Barry Eastmond and Jolyon Skinner.
Zomba Enterprises, Inc., 1990/Barry Eastmond Music, 1990/Jo Skin,
   1990.
Best-selling record by Freddie Jackson on *Do Me Again* (Capitol, 90).

Love Me Two Times
Released by Aerosmith in the film & on the soundtrack LP *Air
   America* (MCA, 90). For copyright information see *Popular Music
   1920-1979*.

Love on Arrival
Words and music by Dan Seals.
Pink Pig Music, 1989.
Best-selling record by Dan Seals from *On Arrival* (Capitol, 89).

Love Takes Time
Words and music by Mariah Carey and Ben Margulies.
Been Jammin', 1990/Vision of Love Songs Inc., 1990.
Best-selling record by Mariah Carey on *Mariah Carey* (Columbia, 90).

Love That Never Dies
Words and music by Roger McGuinn and Stan Lynch.
McGuinn, 1990/Virgin Music, Inc., 1990/Mantanzas Music, 1990.
Introduced by The Byrds on *The Byrds* (Columbia, 90). One of four
   tunes by the original Byrds included in a boxed set chronicling their
   history.

Love under New Management
Words and music by Gabriel Hardeman and Annette Hardeman.
Gabeson, 1989/On the Move, 1989.
Best-selling record by Miki Howard from *Miki Howard* (Atlantic, 89).

Love Will Lead You Back
Words and music by Diane Warren.
Realsongs, 1989.
Best-selling record by Taylor Dayne from *Can't Fight Fate* (Arista, 89).

Love Will Never Do (Without You)
Words and music by James Harris, III and Terry Lewis.
Flyte Tyme Tunes, 1989.
Best-selling record by Janet Jackson in *Rhythm Nation 1814* (A&M,
   89).

Love Without End, Amen
Words and music by Aaron Barker.
O-Tex, 1989/Bill Butler Music.
Best-selling record by George Strait from *Beyond the Blue Neon*
   (MCA, 89).

Lovers in a Dangerous Time (Canadian)
Words and music by Bruce Cockburn.
Golden Mountain Music Inc., 1984.
Revived by Dan Fogelberg on *The Wild Places* (Full Moon/Epic, 90).

M

Make It Like It Was
Words and music by CeCe Winans.
For Our Children, 1989/Zomba Enterprises, Inc., 1989.
Best-selling record by Regina Belle from *Stay with Me* (Columbia, 89).

Make It with You
Revived by Teddy Pendergrass on *Rubaiyat* (Elektra, 90). For
copyright information see *Popular Music 1920-1979*.

Make You Sweat
Words and music by Keith Sweat, Timothy Gatling, and Bobby
Wooten.
WB Music Corp., 1990/E/A/Keith Sweat/REW/Whole Nine
Yards/Vertim.
Best-selling record by Keith Sweat from *I'll Give All My Love to You*
(Elektra, 90).

Mama Will Provide
Words by Lynn Ahrens, music by Stephen Flaherty.
WB Music Corp., 1990/Warner-Tamerlane Publishing
Corp./Hillsdale Music/Stephen Flaherty.
Introduced by Kecia Lewis-Evans and Company in the musical and
original cast album *Once on This Island* (RCA, 90).

Many a Long & Lonesome Highway
Words and music by Rodney Crowell and Will Jennings.
Coolwell Music, 1989/Willin' David/Blue Sky Rider Songs.
Best-selling record Rodney Crowell from *Keys to the Highway*
(Columbia, 89).

March of the Cosmetic Surgeons (English)
Words and music by Richard Thompson.

Beeswing Music, 1990.
Introduced by French Frith Kaiser Thompson on *Invisible Means* (Windham Hill, 90). Track features mezzo soprano Catherine Keen.

The Marching Song of the Covert Battalions (English)
Words and music by Billy Bragg.
Chappell & Co., Inc., 1990.
Introduced by Billy Bragg on *The Internationale* (Elektra/Utility, 90).

Marquee Moon
Words and music by Tom Verlaine.
Double Exposure Music Inc., 1977.
Revived by The Kronos Quartet on *Rubaiyat* (Elektra, 90).

Me & Elvis
Words and music by Ross Rice.
CBS Songs Ltd., London, England, 1990/Hook 'N B/House Projects.
Introduced by Human Radio on *Human Radio* (Columbia, 90).

Me and the Devil Blues
Words and music by Robert Johnson.
King of Spades Music, 1990.
Revived by The Cowboy Junkies in the film and on the soundtrack album *Pump Up the Volume* (MCA, 90).

The Measure of a Man
Words and music by Alan Menken.
United Lion Music Inc., 1990/EMI-Blackwood Music Inc.
Introduced by Elton John in the film and on the soundtrack album *Rocky V* (Bust It/Capitol Records, 90).

Mentirosa (Cuban)
English words and music by Sergio Reyes and Tony Gonzales.
Varry White Music, 1990.
Best-selling record by Mellow Man Ace from *Escape from Havana* (Capitol, 90).

Merry Go Round
Words and music by Keith Sweat and Bobby Douglas.
Keith Sweat, 1990/Bobby D/WB Music Corp./E/A/MCA Music.
Best-selling record by Keith Sweat from *I'll Give All My Love to You* (Vintertainment, 90).

Middle-Aged Blues Boogie
Words and music by Gaya Adegbalola.
Hot Toddy Music, 1990.
Introduced by Saffire in *The Uppity Blues Women* (Alligator, 90). Winner of the W.C. Handy award for Best Blues Song of the Year.

Miles Away
Words and music by Paul Taylor.
Virgin Songs, 1990/Small Hope Music/Paul Taylor.
Best-selling record by Winger from *In the Heart of the Young* (Atlantic, 90).

Miracle (from *Young Guns II*)
Words and music by Jon Bon Jovi.
Bon Jovi Publishing, 1990/PRI Music.
Best-selling record by Jon Bon Jovi from *Blaze of Glory*, the soundtrack to *Young Guns II* (Mercury, 90).

Missunderstanding
Words and music by D.J. Eddie, Frank Nevelle, and Al B. Sure!.
Al B. Sure International, 1990/EMI-April Music Inc./Across 110th Street/Frank Nitty/Velle International/Ness, Nitty & Capone.
Best-selling record by Al B. Sure! from *Private Times...and the Whole 9!* (Warner Bros., 90).

More
Words and music by Stephen Sondheim.
Rilting Music Inc., 1990/WB Music Corp., 1990.
Introduced by Madonna in the film *Dick Tracy* and on the LP *I'm Breathless* (Sire/Warner Bros., 90). The inspired matchup of the theater's premier composer and pop's reigning vamp. Nominated for a Grammy Award, Song for TV or film, 1990.

More Than Words Can Say (Canadian)
Words and music by Freddy Curci and Steve DeMarchi.
Pasta, 1990/De'Mar.
Best-selling record by Alias from *Alias* (EMI, 90).

Mother Earth
Words and music by Neil Young.
Silver Fiddle, 1990.
Introduced by Neil Young & Crazy Horse on *Ragged Glory* (Reprise, 90). Contributing toward the year's environmental consciousness.

The Movie in My Mind (French)
English words and music by Claude-Michel Schonberg, Richard Maltby, Jr., and Alain Boublil.
Alain Boublil Music Inc., 1989.
Performed by Isan Alvarez and Lee Salonga in the original cast LP *Miss Saigon* (Geffen, 90). The long-anticipated opening of the musical was delayed by an actor's equity complaint about casting.

My Finest Hour (English)
Words and music by David Gavurin and Harriet Wheeler.

Geffen Music, 1989/WB Music Corp.
Introduced by The Sundays on *Reading, Writing and Arithmetic* (DGC, 90).

My Kinda Girl
Words and music by L. A. Reid (pseudonym for Antonio Reid), Babyface (pseudonym for Kenny Edmunds), and Darryl Simmons.
Hip-Trip Music Co., 1989/Kear Music/Green Skirt Music.
Best-selling record by Babyface from *Tender Lover* (Solar/Epic, 89).

My Mother the War
Words and music by John Lombardo, Michael Walsh, and Natalie Merchant.
Christian Burial Music, 1983.
Revived by 10,000 Maniacs on *Hope Chest* (Elektra, 90). One of their early anti-war epics.

My, My, My
Words and music by Babyface (pseudonym for Kenny Edmunds) and Darryl Simmons.
Kear Music, 1990/Epic/Solar/Tree Publishing Co., Inc./Green Skirt Music.
Best-selling record by Johnny Gill from *Johnny Gill* (Motown, 90). Nominated for a Grammy Award for Best Rhythm & Blues Song of the Year.

Mysteries of Love
Music by Angelo Badalamenti, words by David Lynch.
Anlon Music Co., 1990/O.K. Paul Music.
Performed by Julee Cruise on the TV series *Twin Peaks* (Warner Bros., 90). Also on Cruise's LP *Floating into the Night* (Warner Bros., 90).

N

The Neighborhood
Words and music by David Hidalgo and Louis Perez.
Davince Music, 1990/No K. O. Music/Bug Music.
Introduced by Los Lobos on *The Neighborhood* (Slash/Warner Bros., 90).

Never Knew Lonely
Words and music by Vince Gill.
Benefit, 1987.
Best-selling record by Vince Gill from *When I Call Your Name* (MCA, 90).

New Blue Moon
Words and music by Traveling Wilburys.
Ganga Publishing Co., 1990/Zero Productions/Special Rider Music/EMI-April Music Inc./Gone Gator Music.
Introduced by The Traveling Wilburys on *The Traveling Wilburys, Vol. 3* (Warner Bros., 90).

Next Time
Words by Richard Maltby, Jr., music by David Shire.
Fiddleback Music Publishing Co., Inc., 1985/Progeny Music, 1985/Revelation Music Publishing Corp., 1985/Long Pond Music, 1985.
Revived by Patrick Brady on *Closer Than Ever* (MCA, 90). Originally written for the musical *Love Match*. Sung as a medley with "I Wouldn't Go Back."

Next to You, Next to Me
Words and music by Russell Ellis Orrall and Curtis Wright.
BMG Music, 1990/2 Kids/David N. Will.
Best-selling record by Shenandoah from *Extra Mile* (Columbia, 90).

Nick and Nora
Music by Charles Strouse, words by Richard Maltby, Jr.
Fiddleback Music Publishing Co., Inc., 1990.
Introduced by Charles Strouse and Richard Maltby, Jr. at the 18th
  annual spring gala of the Manhattan Theater Club. Tune is the title
  of a forthcoming Broadway musical.

The Nightingale
Music by Angelo Badalamenti, words by David Lynch.
Anlon Music Co., 1990/O.K. Paul Music.
Introduced by Julee Cruise on *Floating into the Night* (Warner Bros.,
  90). Also on the TV show & soundtrack LP *Twin Peaks* (Warner
  Bros., 90).

1959
Words and music by Bill Bonk.
Figaro Music, 1990.
Introduced by The Brothers Figaro on *Gypsy Beat* (Geffen, 90).

No Man's Land (English)
Words and music by Eric Bogle.
Larrikin Music, 1976/Music Sales Corp.
Revived by Peter, Paul & Mary on *Flowers and Stones* (Cold Castle,
  90).

No Matter How High
Words and music by Even Stevens and Joey Scarbury.
ESP Management Inc., 1989.
Best-selling record by the Oak Ridge Boys from *American Dreams*
  (MCA, 89).

No More Lies
Words and music by L.A. Dre (pseudonym for Andre Bolton),
  Michel'le, and Laylaw.
Ruthless Attack Muzick, 1989.
Best-selling record by Michel'le from *Michel'le* (Atco, 89).

No Myth
Words and music by Michael Penn.
Liafail, 1989/Careers Music Inc.
Best-selling record by Michael Penn from *March* (RCA, 89). Penn's
  brother is the actor Sean.

Nobody But You
Words and music by Lou Reed and John Cale.
Metal Machine Music, 1989/John Cale, 1989.
Introduced by Lou Reed and John Cale from *Songs for Drella* (Sire,
  90). Cale, John.

Nobody's Talking
Words and music by Randy Sharp and Sonny Lemaire.
With Any Luck Music, 1988/Sun Mare Music Publishing.
Best-selling record by Exile from *Still Standing* (Arista, 90).

Not Counting You
Words and music by Garth Brooks.
Major Bob Music, 1989.
Best-selling record by Garth Brooks from *Garth Brooks* (Capitol, 89).

Nothing Compares 2 U
Words and music by Prince Rogers Nelson.
Controversy Music, 1985/WB Music Corp.
Revived by Sinead O'Connor from *I Do Not Want What I Haven't Got*
   (Chrysalis, 90). Originally recorded by Prince. Nominated for
   Grammy Awards for Best Song of the Year and Best Record of the
   Year.

Nothing Ever Happens (Scottish)
Words and music by Justin Currie.
Theobalds, 1990.
Introduced by Del Amitri in *Waking Hours* (A&M, 90).

Nothing's News
Words and music by Clint Black.
Howlin' Hits Music, 1988.
Best-selling record by Clint Black from *Killin' Time* (RCA, 89).

November Spawned a Monster (English)
Words and music by Morrissey and Clive Langer.
Bona Relations Music, 1990/Warner-Tamerlane Publishing Corp.,
   1900/Copyright Control.
Introduced by Morrissey on *Bona Drag* (Sire, 90).

Now That I Am Dead (English)
Words and music by Donna Blair and John French.
J. French Music, 1990.
Introduced by French Frith Kaiser Thompson on *Invisible Means*
   (Windham Hill, 90).

O

Oh Black Pool (English)
Words and music by Paul Heaton and David Rotheray.
Go! Discs Ltd., England, 1989.
The Beautiful South from *Welcome to the Beautiful South* (Elektra, 90).

Oh Father
Words and music by Madonna Ciccone and Patrick Leonard.
WB Music Corp., 1989/Bleu Disque Music/Webo Girl Music/WB Music Corp./Johnny Yuma.
Best-selling record by Madonna from *Like a Prayer* (Sire, 89).

Oh Girl
Revived by Paul Young from *Other Voices* (Columbia, 90). For copyright information, see *Popular Music 1920-1979*.

Oi! It's So Humid
Words and music by Joe Stone and Eric Lambert.
Pac Jam Publishing, 1990.
Introduced by 2 Live Jews on *As Kosher as They Wanna Be*. A parody of 2 Live Crew's "Me So Horny."

Old Friend
Words and music by Loudon Wainwright.
Frank Music Co., 1971.
Revived by Marti Jones on *Any Kind of Lie* (BMG, 90).

On a Night Like This
Words and music by Fred Koller.
Lucrative, 1990.
Introduced by Fred Koller on *Where the Fast Lane Ends* (Alcazar, 90).

On Second Thought
Words and music by Eddie Rabbitt.

Eddie Rabbitt Music Publishing, 1989.
Best-selling record by Eddie Rabbitt from *Jersey Boy* (Capitol, 89).

On the Greener Side
Words and music by Michelle Shocked.
Polygram Songs, 1989.
Best-selling record by Michelle Shocked from *Captain Swing* (Mercury, 90).

Once in a While
Words and music by Richard O'Brian.
Hallenbeck Music Co., 1974.
Recorded by Barry Bostwick for *The Rocky Horror Picture Show* but never released. Surfaces on *The Rocky Horror Picture Show 15th Anniversary Collection* (Rhino, 90).

One and Only Man (English)
Words and music by Steve Winwood and Jim Capaldi.
F.S. Ltd., England, 1990/Warner-Tamerlane Publishing Corp./Freedom/Warner-Chappell Music.
Best-selling record by Steve Winwood from *Refugees of the Heart* (Virgin, 90).

One More Parade
Words and music by Phil Ochs and Bob Gibson.
Warner Brothers, Inc., 1964.
Revived by They Might Be Giants on *Rubaiyat* (Elektra, 90).

One of the Good Guys
Words by Richard Maltby, Jr., music by David Shire.
Fiddleback Music Publishing Co., Inc., 1987/Progeny Music, 1987/Revelation Music Publishing Corp., 1987/Long Pond Music, 1987.
Revived by Brent Barrett on the original cast album of *Closer Than Ever* (RCA, 90). Originally written for the musical *Urban Blight.*

The One That Got Away
Words and music by John Gorka.
Blues Palace, 1990.
Introduced by John Gorka on *Land of the Bottom Line* (Windham Hill, 90).

Ooh La La (I Can't Get over You)
Words and music by Maurice Starr.
EMI-April Music Inc., 1990/Maurice Starr Music.
Best-selling record by Perfect Gentlemen from *Rated PG* (Columbia, 90).

Open House
Words and music by Lou Reed and John Cale.
Metal Machine Music, 1989/John Cale.
Introduced by Lou Reed and John Cale in *Songs for Drella* (Sire, 90).

Opening Act
Words and music by Mary Chapin Carpenter.
EMI-April Music Inc., 1990/Getarealjob Music.
Introduced by Mary Chapin Carpenter at the Country Music Awards
　Show, when this caustic tune brought down the house.

Opposites Attract
Words and music by Oliver Leiber.
Virgin Songs, 1989/Oliver Leiber Music.
Best-selling record by Paula Abdul (duet with the Wild Pair) on
　Forever Your Girl (Virgin, 89). Fourth #1 single from her album.
　Ushered in a dance-crazy year.

P

Papa Was a Rolling Stone
Revived by Was (Not Was) in *Are You Okay* (Chrysalis, 90). For
 copyright information see *Popular Music 1920-1979*.

Pass It on Down
Words and music by Teddy Gentry, Randy Owen, Will Robinson,
 and Ronnie Rogers.
Maypop Music, 1990.
Best-selling record by Alabama from *Pass It on Down* (RCA, 90).

Paths of Victory
Words and music by Bob Dylan.
Warner Brothers, Inc., 1964.
Revived by The Byrds on *The Byrds* (Columbia, 90). Classic Dylan
 tune recorded by his early compatriots, who brought "Mr.
 Tambourine Man" to the top in 1965.

Peace in Our Time (English)
Words and music by Andy Hill and Pete Sinfield.
Pillarview, 1988/Chrysalis Music Corp./Virgin Songs.
Best-selling record by Eddie Money from *Greatest Hits...Sound of
 Money* (Columbia, 89).

Personal Jesus (English)
Words and music by Martin Gore.
Emile Music, 1990.
Best-selling record by Depeche Mode from *Violator* (Sire, 90).

Phonograph Blues
Words and music by Robert Johnson.
King of Spades Music, 1990.
Performed by Robert Johnson on *The Complete Recordings* (Columbia,
 90).

Picture of Helen
Words and music by Walter Salas-Humera.
Voltone, 1990/Music Corp. of America, 1990.
Introduced by The Silos on *The Silos* (RCA, 90).

Pictures in the Hallway
Words and music by Craig Carnelia.
Frank Music Co., 1990.
Performed by Maureen Silliman in the revue *Pictures in the Hallway*.

Pictures of You (English)
Words and music by Robert Smith, Simon Gallup, Boris Williams,
    Purl Thompson, Roger O'Donnell, and Laurence Tolhurst.
Fiction Music Inc., 1989.
Introduced by The Cure from *Disintegration* (Elektra, 89).

Planet Love
Words and music by Gerome Ragni, James Rado, and Galt
    MacDermot.
Introduced by the authors Rado, Ragni & MacDermot at a preview of
    their forthcoming musical *Sun*.

Planet Schmanet Janet
Words and music by Richard O'Brian.
Hallenbeck Music Co., 1974.
Performed by Tim Curry & Company in *The Rocky Horror Picture
Show 15th Anniversary Collection*. Originally introduced in the movie
but not used on the soundtrack album.

Poison
Words and music by Elliot Straite.
Hi-Frost, 1990.
Best-selling record by Bell Biv Devoe from *Poison* (MCA, 89).

Policy of Truth (English)
Words and music by Martin Gore.
Emile Music, 1990.
Best-selling record by Depeche Mode from *Violator* (Sire/Reprise, 90).

Pollywanacraka
Words and music by Chuck D (pseudonym for Charles Ridenhour).
Def American Songs, 1990/Your Mother's.
Introduced by Public Enemy on *Fear of a Black Planet* (Def
Jam/Columbia, 90).

Post Post Modern Man
Words and music by Mark Mothersbaugh and Gerald V. Casale.

Virgin Music, Inc., 1990/Devo Music.
Introduced by Devo on *Smooth Noodle Maps* (Enigma, 90).

The Power (English)
Words and music by Benito Benites, John Garrett, III, Deron Butler, and Toni C.
Intersong, USA Inc., 1990/Fellow/Songs of Logic/House of Fun Music.
Best-selling record by Snap from *World Power* (Arista, 90). After a cover battle with Chill Rob G, group came under fire for gay-bashing.

Pray
Words and music by Prince Rogers Nelson and M. C. Hammer.
Controversy Music, 1990/WB Music Corp./Bust It Publishing.
Best-selling record by M. C. Hammer in *Please Hammer Don't Hurt 'Em* (Capitol, 90).

Praying for Time (English)
Words and music by George Michael.
Morrison Leahy, England, 1990/Chappell & Co., Inc.
Best-selling record by George Michael from *Listen Without Prejudice, Vol. 1* (Columbia, 90). Song adopted by U.S. troops in Iraq to epitomize their feelings before the war started.

Prelude to a Kiss
Revived as theme music in the play *Prelude to a Kiss*. For copyright information see *Popular Music 1920-1979*.

Price of Love
Words and music by John Waite and Jonathan Cain.
Wild Crusade, 1989/Frisco Kid Music/Chappell & Co., Inc.
Best-selling record by Bad English from *Bad English* (Epic, 89).

Problem Child
Words and music by Terry Melcher.
Music Corp. of America, 1990/Daywin Music, Inc./Clairaudient.
Introduced by The Beach Boys in the film *Problem Child*. Released as a single (RCA, 90).

Promise Me You'll Remember (Love Theme from *The Godfather III*)
Words by John Bettis, music by Carmine Coppola.
John Bettis Music, 1990/Famous Music Corp./Carmit.
Introduced by Harry Connick, Jr. in the film and soundtrack LP *The Godfather III* (Columbia, 90). Nominated for Academy Award, Best Original Song, 1990.

Put the Message in the Box (Irish)
Words and music by Karl Wallinger.
Polygram International, 1990.
Introduced by World Party on *Goodbye Jumbo* (Chrysalis, 90).

Put Yourself in My Shoes
Words and music by Clint Black, Hayden Nicholas, and Shake
 Russell.
Howlin' Hits Music, 1989/Red Brazos.
Introduced by Clint Black on *Put Yourself in My Shoes* (RCA, 90).
 Performed for the first time on the Country Music Awards TV
 Show.

R

Razor Blades of Love (Scottish)
Words and music by Jimmie O'Neill.
Introduced by The Silencers on *A Blues for Buddah* (RCA, 89).

Ready or Not
Words and music by L. A. Reid (pseudonym for Antonio Reid) and
    Babyface (pseudonym for Kenny Edmunds).
Epic/Solar, 1989/Kear Music.
Best-selling record by After 7 from *After 7* (Virgin, 89).

Real Love
Words and music by Solomon Roberts.
Skyyzoo Songs, 1989.
Best-selling record Skyy from *Start of a New Romance* (Atlantic, 89).

Real World
Words and music by Bruce Springsteen.
Bruce Springsteen Publishing, 1990.
Introduced by Bruce Springsteen at the Shrine Auditorium in Los
    Angeles.

Red-Headed Woman (Sure Gets the Dirty Job Done)
Words and music by Bruce Springsteen.
Bruce Springsteen Publishing, 1990.
Introduced by Bruce Springsteen in performance at the Shrine
    Auditorium in Los Angeles.

Red Red Rose
Words and music by David Mallett.
Music Sales Corp., 1990/EMI-April Music Inc.
Introduced by Emmylou Harris on *Brand New Dance* (Reprise, 90).

Release Me
Words and music by Wilson Phillips.

EMI-Blackwood Music Inc., 1989/Wilphill.
Best-selling record by Wilson Phillips from *Wilson Phillips* (SBK, 90).

Remember When the Music
Words and music by Harry Chapin.
Story Songs Ltd., 1980.
Revived by Bruce Springsteen on *Harry Chapin Tribute* (Relativity, 90). A 1987 concert in tribute to the singer/songwriter/activist, who died in 1981.

The Rest of the Dream
Words and music by John Hiatt.
Whistling Moon Traveler, 1990/Careers Music Inc.
Introduced by John Hiatt on *Stolen Moments* (A&M, 90).

Revolutionary Generation
Words and music by Chuck D (pseudonym for Charles Ridenhour), Flavor Flav (pseudonym for William Drayton), and Terminator X (pseudonym for Norman Rogers).
Def American Songs, 1990/Your Mother's.
Introduced by Public Enemy on *Fear of a Black Planet* (Def Jam/Columbia, 90).

Richest Man on Earth
Words and music by Paul Overstreet and Don Schlitz.
Scarlet Moon Music, 1989/Don Schlitz Music/Almo Music Corp.
Best-selling record by Paul Overstreet from *Sowin' Love* (RCA, 89).

Road to Cairo
Words and music by David Ackles.
Warner-Tamerlane Publishing Corp., 1968.
Revived by Howard Jones on *Rubaiyat* (Elektra, 90).

Roam
Words and music by B-52's and Robert Waldrop.
Man Woman Together Now Music, 1989/Irving Music Inc.
Best-selling record by The B-52's from *Cosmic Thing* (Reprise, 89).

Romeo
Words and music by Dino.
Island Music, 1990/Onid Music/Willesden Music, Inc./Doc Ice.
Best-selling record by Dino from *Swingin'* (Island, 90).

Room at the Top (English)
Words and music by Adam Ant, Marco Pirroni, and Andre Cymone.
Colgems-EMI Music Inc., 1989/EMI-April Music Inc./Ultrawave.
Best-selling record by Adam Ant from *Manners & Physique* (MCA, 90).

Round and Round
Words and music by Prince Rogers Nelson.
Controversy Music, 1990/WB Music Corp.
Best-selling record by Tevin Campbell in the film and soundtrack of
  Graffiti Bridge (Paisley Park, 90).

Rub You the Right Way
Words and music by James Harris, III and Terry Lewis.
Flyte Tyme Tunes, 1990.
Best-selling record by Johnny Gill from *Johnny Gill* (Motown, 90).

Runagate Runagate
Words and music by Wendell Logan.
Performed by William Brown with Columbia College Chicago's Black
  Music Repertory Ensemble as part of a program spanning a history
  of black music.

S

Sacrifice (English)
Words and music by Elton John and Bernie Taupin.
Big Pig Music, Ltd., London, England, 1989/Intersong, USA Inc.
Best-selling record by Elton John from *Sleeping with the Past* (MCA, 89).

The Scene of the Crime
Words and music by Dennis Linde.
Linde Manor Publishing Co., 1990.
Introduced by Jo-el Sonnier on *Have a Little Faith* (MCA, 90).

Searching for a Heart
Words and music by Warren Zevon.
Donna Dijon, 1990/Zevon Music Inc./Next Decade.
Introduced by Warren Zevon in the film and on the soundtrack *Love at Large* (Movie Music, 90).

The Secret Garden
Words and music by Quincy Jones, Rod Temperton, Snuff Garrett, and El Debarge.
Hee Bee Dooinit, 1989/WB Music Corp./Rodsongs/Almo Music Corp./Black Chick/Rambush.
Best-selling record by Quincy Jones from *Back on the Block* (Warner Bros, 89).

Secret Silken World
Words and music by David Baerwald.
Introduced by David Baerwald but not included on his solo album.

Seein' My Father in Me
Words and music by Paul Overstreet and Taylor Dunn.
Scarlet Moon Music, 1989.
Best-selling record by Paul Overstreet from *Sowin' Love* (RCA, 89).

Sending All My Love (Turkish)
English words and music by Tolga Katas and Charlie Pennachio.
Turkishman, 1990/Pennachio.
Best-selling record by Linear from *Linear* (Atlantic, 90).

Sensitive New Age Guys
Words and music by Christine Lavin and John Gorka.
Flip a Jig, 1989/Blues Palace.
Introduced by Christine Lavin on *Attainable Love* (Philo, 90).

Sensitivity
Words and music by James Harris, III and Terry Lewis.
Flyte Tyme Tunes, 1990.
Best-selling record by Ralph Tresvant from *Ralph Tresvant* (MCA, 90).

Seven & Seven Is
Words and music by Arthur Lee.
Grass Root Productions, 1966.
Revived by Billy Bragg on *Rubaiyat* (Elektra, 90).

7 Deadly Sins
Words and music by Traveling Wilburys.
Ganga Publishing Co., 1990/Zero Productions/Special Rider
    Music/EMI-April Music Inc./Gone Gator Music.
Introduced by The Traveling Wilburys on *The Traveling Wilburys, Vol.
    3* (Warner Bros., 90). A do-wop send-up in folk/rock style.

Shave Your Legs (Canadian)
Words and music by Moe Berg.
EMI April Canada, 1990/Pursuit of Tunes.
Introduced by Pursuit of Happiness on *One-Sided Story* (Chrysalis, 90).

She Ain't Worth It
Words and music by Antonia Armato, Ian Prince, and Bobby Brown.
Tom Sturges, 1990/Chrysalis Music Corp./Bobby Brown/Unicity
    Music, Inc./EMI-April Music Inc.
Best-selling record by Glenn Medeiros featuring Bobby Brown from
    Glenn Medeiros (MCA, 90).

She Came from Fort Worth
Words and music by Pat Alger and Fred Koller.
Bait and Beer, 1989/Forerunner/Lucrative/Bug Music/Coburn.
Best-selling record by Kathy Mattea from *Willow in the Wind*
    (Mercury, 89).

The Shoop Shoop Song (It's in His Kiss)
Revived by Cher in the film and on the soundtrack album *Mermaids*
    (Geffen, 90). For copyright information see *Popular Music*

1920-1979. Song is the centerpiece of the play *Mama, I Want to Sing II,* which is the story of Doris Troy, who sang the original hit in 1963.

Short Stop
Words and music by Sara Hickman.
Esta Chica, 1990/Music Corp. of America.
Introduced by Sara Hickman on *Shortstop* (Elektra, 90).

Show Me
Words and music by Jan Nettlesbey, Terry Coffey, and Howard Hewett.
WB Music Corp., 1990/E/A/Make It Big/Chicago Brothers Music/Warner-Tamerlane Publishing Corp.
Best-selling record by Howard Hewett from *Howard Hewett* (Elektra, 90).

Show Me Heaven
Words and music by Hans Zimmer.
Ensign Music Corp., 1990.
Introduced by Maria McKee in the film and on the soundtrack album *Days of Heaven* (Geffen, 90).

Show Me to the Top (Irish)
Words and music by Karl Wallinger.
Polygram International, 1990.
Introduced by World Party on *Goodbye Jumbo* (Chrysalis, 90).

Sittin' in the Lap of Luxury
Words and music by Louie Louie and Les Pierce.
Louie Louie Entertainment/CRGI/Lorna Lee.
Best-selling record by Louie Louie from *The State I'm In* (Epic, 90).
    Trumpet solo by Dizzy Gillespie.

Sleigh Ride
Words and music by James Harris, III and Terry Lewis.
Flyte Tyme Tunes, 1990.
Introduced by The Chipmunks on *Rockin' Through the Decades* (EMI, 90).

Slip Away (A Warning)
Words and music by Lou Reed and John Cale.
Metal Machine Music, 1989/John Cale.
Introduced by Lou Reed and John Cale on *Songs for Drella* (Sire, 90).

Slow Motion
Words and music by Stanley Sheppard and Aaron Smith.

Stanton's Gold, 1990/Island Music/Tracye One/Maypop Music.
Best-selling record by Gerald Alston from *Open Invitation* (Motown, 90).

Smalltown
Words and music by Lou Reed.
Metal Machine Music, 1989/John Cale.
Introduced by Lou Reed and John Cale on *Songs for Drella* (Sire, 90).

Smoke on the Mountain
Words and music by Alan Bailey.
Introduced by the cast of the musical *Smoke on the Mountain* (90).

So Close
Words and music by Daryl Hall, George Green, Danny Kortchmar, and Jon Bon Jovi.
Hot Cha Music Co., 1990/Careers Music Inc./Full Keel/EEG Music/Kortchmar Music/New Jersey Underground/Polygram International.
Best-selling record by Daryl Hall and John Oates from *Change of Season* (Arista, 90).

So You Like What You See (English)
Words and music by Thom McElroy, Denzil Foster, and Samuelle.
Two Tuff-Enuff Publishing, 1990/Irving Music Inc.
Best-selling record by Samuelle from *Living in Black Paradise* (Atlantic, 90).

Some People's Lives
Words and music by Janis Ian and Rhonda Fleming.
Irving Music Inc., 1990/Mine Music, Ltd.
Introduced by Bette Midler on *Some People's Lives* (Atlantic, 90).

Some Wings
Music by Maurice Jarre, words by Ray Underwood.
Famous Music Corp., 1990.
Introduced by Vanessa Williams in the film *Almost an Angel* (90).

Someday
Words and music by Bob Merrill.
Chappell & Co., Inc., 1990.
Introduced in the musical *Hannah...1939*.

Someone Keeps Moving My Chair
Words and music by They Might Be Giants.
They Might Be Giants Music, 1989.
Introduced by They Might Be Giants on *Flood* (Elektra, 90).

Someone Like You (English)
Music by Frank Wildhorn, words by Leslie Bricusse.
Stage-Screen Music, Inc., 1990/Cherry Lane Music Co.,
Inc./Scaramanga Music.
Introduced by Linda Eder in the musical and cast album of *Jekyll &
Hyde* (RCA, 90).

Something Happened on the Way to Heaven (English)
Words and music by Phil Collins and Daryl Stuermer.
Phil Collins, England, 1989/Hit & Run Music.
Best-selling record by Phil Collins from *...But Seriously* (Atlantic, 89).

Something Is Happening
Words and music by William Finn.
Introduced by Heather MacRae in the musical *Return to Falsettoland*
(90).

Something to Believe In
Words and music by Bobby Dall, C. C. DeVille, Bret Michaels, and
Rikki Rockett.
Sweet Cyanide, 1990/Willesden Music, Inc.
Best-selling record by Poison from *Flesh and Blood* (Enigma, 90).

Something Wild
Words and music by John Hiatt.
Lillybilly, 1990/Bug Music.
Introduced by Iggy Pop on *Brick by Brick* (Virgin, 90).

Sometimes She Cries
Words and music by Jani Lane.
Virgin Songs, 1989/Dick Dragon Music/Crab Salad Music/Likete
Split Music/Rich McBitch Music/Great Lips Music.
Best-selling record by Warrant from *Dirty Rotten Filthy Stinking Rich*
(Columbia, 89).

Somewhere in My Memory (American-English)
Words by Leslie Bricusse, music by John Williams.
Fox Film Music Corp., 1990.
Introduced by The Boston Pops Orchestra and Choir, conducted by
John Williams in the film *Home Alone*. Nominated for an Academy
Award, Best Original Song, 1990.

Song for Whoever (English)
Words and music by Paul Heaton and David Rotheray.
Go! Discs Ltd., England, 1989.
Introduced by The Beautiful South on *Welcome to the Beautiful South*
(Elektra, 90).

Sooner or Later (I Always Get My Man)
Words and music by Stephen Sondheim.
Rilting Music Inc., 1990/WB Music Corp.
Introduced by Madonna in the film *Dick Tracy* and on the LP *I'm Breathless* (Sire/Warner Bros., 90). Nominated for a Grammy Award for Best Song for TV or film. Winner of an Academy Award, Best Original Song, 1990.

Soul Driver
Words and music by Bruce Springsteen.
Bruce Springsteen Publishing, 1990.
Introduced by Bruce Springsteen at the Shrine Auditorium in Los Angeles.

Southern Star
Words and music by Roger Murrah, Steve Dean, and Rich Alves.
Tom Collins Music Corp., 1985/Collins Court Music, Inc.
Best-selling record by Alabama from *Southern Star* (RCA, 89).

Southland in the Springtime
Words and music by Emily Saliers.
Godhap Music, 1990/Virgin Songs.
Introduced by The Indigo Girls on *Indians* (Epic, 90).

Souvenir
Words by Edna St. Vincent Millay, music by Ricky Ian Gordon.
Introduced by Angelina Reaux in *Sweet Song*, a one-woman concert. Song based on text by poet Edna St. Vincent Millay.

Spirit Voices (American-Argentinian)
Portuguese words by Milton Nascimento, English words and music by Paul Simon.
Paul Simon Music, 1989.
Introduced by Paul Simon on *The Rhythm of the Saints* (Warner Bros., 90). Arranged by Vincent Nguini, based on a traditional Ghanian song, "Yaa Amponsah," by Jacob Sam.

Spread My Wings
Words and music by Chuckii Booker.
Selessongs, 1989/Sarapis.
Best-selling record by Troop from *Attitude* (Atlantic, 89).

Stand Up (Love in the Corners) (Canadian)
Words and music by Ferron.
Nemesis, 1990.
Introduced by Ferron on *Phantom Center* (Chameleon, 90).

Statue of a Fool
Words and music by Jerry Crutchfield.
Sure Fire Music Co., Inc., 1988.
Best-selling record by Ricky Van Shelton from *Loving Proof* (Columbia, 88).

Step by Step
Words and music by Maurice Starr.
Maurice Starr Music, 1989/EMI-April Music Inc.
Best-selling record by New Kids on the Block from *Step by Step* (Columbia, 89).

Stop Your Crying
Words and music by Bob Mould.
Granary Music, 1990.
Introduced by Bob Mould on *Black Sheets of Rain* (Virgin, 90).

Straight in at 37 (English)
Words and music by David Rotheray and Paul Heaton.
Go! Discs Ltd., England, 1989.
Introduced by The Beautiful South in *Welcome to the Beautiful South* (Elektra, 90).

Stranded
Words and music by J. Kyle and J. Harrington.
Wrensong, 1990.
Best-selling record by Heart from *Brigade* (Capitol, 90).

Stranger
Words and music by David Baerwald.
Zen of Iniquity, 1990/Almo Music Corp.
Introduced by David Baerwald on *Bedtime Stories* (A&M, 90).

Stranger Things Have Happened
Words and music by Keith Stegall and Roger Murrah.
Tom Collins Music Corp., 1989/Murrah.
Best-selling record by Ronnie Milsap on *Ronnie Milsap* (RCA, 90).

Strawberry Fields Forever (English)
Revived by Candy Flip (Atlantic, 90). For copyright info, see *Popular Music 1920-1979*.

Style It Takes
Words and music by Lou Reed and John Cale.
Metal Machine Music, 1989/John Cale.
Introduced by Lou Reed and John Cale on *Songs for Drella* (Sire, 90).

Suicide Blonde (Australian)
Words and music by Andrew Farriss and Michael Hutchence.
Tol Muziek, 1990.
Best-selling record Inxs from *X* (Atlantic, 90).

Sun Won't Stop
Words and music by Holly Hear and Steve Wood.
Hereford, 1989/Albedo.
Introduced by Holly Near on *Sky Dances* (Redwood, 90).

Sunflower
Words and music by Bill Bonk and Phil Parlapiano.
Figaro Music, 1989.
Introduced by The Brothers Figaro on *Gypsy Beat* (Geffen, 90).

Sunken City (Canadian)
Words and music by Ferron.
Nemesis, 1989.
Introduced by Ferron on *Phantom Center* (Chameleon, 90).

Superfly 1990
Words and music by Curtis Mayfield.
M, M&M, 1990.
Revived by Curtis Mayfield & Ice-T in the film & soundtrack LP
Return of Superfly (Capitol, 90). On the brink of a major comeback,
Mayfield was seriously injured in a freak stage accident.

Sweet Soul Dream (Irish)
Words and music by Karl Wallinger.
Polygram International, 1990.
Introduced by World Party on *Goodbye Jumbo* (Ensign/Chrysalis, 90).

Swing
Words and music by Rupert Holmes.
Holmes Line of Music, 1990.
Introduced by Rupert Holmes at a cabaret show in NYC prior to the
upcoming Broadway opening of *Swing*.

The Sword of Damocles
Words and music by Richard O'Brian.
Hallenbeck Music Co., 1974.
Introduced by Peter Hinwood in the movie and collected on the album
The Rocky Horror Picture Show 15th Anniversary Collection (Rhino,
90).

T

Tell Me Why
Words and music by Lewis Martinee.
EMI Music Publishing, Ltd., London, England, 1989/Panchin.
Best-selling record Expose from *What You Don't Know* (Arista, 89).

Tender Lover
Words and music by Babyface (pseudonym for Kenny Edmunds), L.
    A. Reid (pseudonym for Antonio Reid), and Pete Q. Smith.
Hip-Trip Music Co., 1989/Kear Music/Jenn-a-Bug Music.
Best-selling record by Babyface from *Tender Lover* (Solar, 89).

Thank You World (Soviet)
English words and music by Karl Wallinger.
Polygram International, 1990.
Introduced by World Party on *Goodbye Jumbo* (Ensign/Chrysalis, 90).

There's Always Love (Soviet)
English words and music by Michael Bolton, Desmond Child, Albert
    Hammond, Holly Knight, Brenda Russell, Diane Warren, and
    Vladimir Matetsky.
EMI-April Music Inc., 1990/Is Hot Music, Ltd./Desmobile Music
    Co./Albert Hammond/Colgems-EMI Music Inc./Knighty
    Knight/Geffen Music/Rutland Road/Realsongs/WB Music
    Corp./Taurus Music.
Introduced by Patti LaBelle on *Music Speaks Louder Than Words*
    (Epic, 90), a collaboration between the top songwriters of the U.S.
    and Soviet Union.

These Days
Words and music by Jackson Browne.
Companion, 1973/Open Window Music Co.
Revived by 10,000 Maniacs on *Rubaiyat* (Elektra, 90).

Thieves in the Temple
Words and music by Prince Rogers Nelson.
Controversy Music, 1990/WB Music Corp.
Best-selling record by Prince from the film and soundtrack *Graffiti Bridge* (Paisley Park, 90).

Thirty Years of Tears
Words and music by John Hiatt.
Whistling Moon Traveler, 1990/Careers Music Inc.
Introduced by John Hiatt on *Stolen Moments* (A&M, 90).

This Is the Moment (English)
Music by Frank Wildhorn, words by Leslie Bricusse.
Stage & Screen Music Inc., 1990/Cherry Lane Music Co.,
    Inc./Scaramanga Music.
Introduced by Linda Eder and Colm Wilkinson in the musical *Jekyll & Hyde* and on the cast album *Highlights from Jekyll & Hyde* (RCA, 90).

This Is What We Do
Words and music by M. C. Hammer.
Bust It Publishing, 1990/EMI-Blackwood Music Inc.
Introduced by M.C. Hammer in the film and on the soundtrack album *Teenage Mutant Ninja Turtles* (SBK, 90).

This Old Heart of Mine
Revived by Rod Stewart with Ronald Isley from *Downtown Train/Selections from the Storyteller Anthology* (Warner Bros., 89). For copyright information see *Popular Music 1920-1979*.

Through This Vale of Tears
Words and music by David Baker.
Performed by William Brown with Columbia College Chicago's Black Music Repertory Ensemble. A memorial for Martin Luther King.

Through Your Hands
Words and music by John Hiatt.
Whistling Moon Traveler, 1989/Careers Music Inc.
Introduced by John Hiatt on *Stolen Moments* (A&M, 90).

Tic-Tac-Toe
Words and music by Kyper.
RSK, 1990/XTC.
Best-selling record by Kyper from *Tic-Tac-Toe* (Atlantic, 90).

'Til a Tear Becomes a Rose
Words and music by Bill Rice and Mary Sharon Rice.

EMI-April Music Inc., 1983/Swallowfork Music, Inc.
Introduced by Keith Whitley and Lorrie Morgan on *Keith Whitley's Greatest Hits* (RCA, 90).

Till I Can't Take It
Words and music by Clyde Otis and Dorian Burton.
Alley Music, 1968/Trio Music Co., Inc./Eden Music, Inc.
Revived by Billy Joe Royal from *Tell It Like It Is* (Atlantic, 89).

Time of Change
Words and music by Andy Robinson and Betsy Gerson.
Brontosaurus, 1990/Miss Boo.
Introduced by Different World on *Different World* (Vanguard, 90).

Time of the Season (English)
Revived by Wendy Wall on *China Beach--Music and Memories* (SBK, 90). For copyright information, see *Popular Music 1920-1979*.

Times Like This
Words by Lynn Ahrens, music by Stephen Flaherty.
WB Music Corp., 1988/Warner-Tamerlane Publishing Corp., 1988/Hillsdale Music, 1988/Stephen Flaherty, 1988.
Revived in *Lucky Stiff* at the Olney Theater in Washington, D.C. Winner of the Helen Hayes Award for best musical. Introduced by Julie White in the 1988 production at Playwright's Horizon, which won the Richard Rodgers Award.

To Be Young
Words and music by Val Haymes.
Point Barrow, 1990/Music Corp. of America.
Introduced by Lonesome Val on *Lonesome Val* (Restless/Bar None, 90). Winner of Best Song award at the New York Music Awards.

To Where I Am Now (Netherlands)
English words and music by Marty Willson-Piper.
Funzalo Music, 1989.
Revived by Marty Willson-Piper on *Songs from the Sacred Napkin* (Rykodisc, 90).

Tomorrow (A Better You, Better Me)
Words and music by George Johnson, Louis Johnson, and Snuff Garrett.
Kidada Music Inc., 1989/Warner-Tamerlane Publishing Corp./Hee Bee Dooinit/WB Music Corp./Black Chick.
Best-selling record by Quincy Jones with Tevin Campbell from *Back on the Block* (Warner Bros., 89).

Tom's Diner
Words and music by Suzanne Vega.
AGF Music Ltd., 1987/Waifersongs Ltd.
Revived by Suzanne Vega with new production by DNA, from *Solitude Standing* (A&M, 87). Featured on *Jam Harder* (A&M, 90). A pumped up version of Vega's tone poem became a rap hit in England and then in the U.S.

Tonight
Words and music by Maurice Starr and Al Lancellotti.
Maurice Starr Music, 1989/EMI-April Music Inc./Al Lancellotti.
Best-selling record by New Kids on the Block from *Tonight* (Columbia, 89).

Too Cold at Home
Words and music by Bobby Harden.
EMI-April Music Inc., 1990/K-Mark.
Best-selling record by Mark Chestnutt in *Too Cold at Home* (MCA, 90).

Too Late to Say Goodbye
Words and music by Richard Marx and Fee Waybill.
Chi-Boy, 1989/Fee Music.
Best-selling record by Richard Marx from *Repeat Offender* (EMI, 89).

Transverse City
Words and music by Warren Zevon.
Zevon Music Inc., 1990.
Introduced by Warren Zevon on *Transverse City* (Virgin, 90).

Trouble with Classicists
Words and music by Lou Reed and John Cale.
Metal Machine Music, 1989/John Cale.
Introduced by Lou Reed and John Cale on *Songs for Drella* (Sire, 90).

Try Me
Words and music by Full Force.
Forceful Music, 1990/Willesden Music, Inc./My My Music.
Introduced by Jasmine Guy on *Jasmine Guy* (Warner Bros., 90). One of the leads on the TV series *A Different World*.

Turtle Power
Words and music by James Alpern and Richard Usher, Jr.
EMI-Blackwood Music Inc., 1990/Kikinit.
Best-selling record by Partners in Kryme from the film & soundtrack LP *Teenage Mutant Ninja Turtles* (SBK, 90). One of the major kid-crazes of the year.

U

U Can't Touch This
Words and music by Rick James, James Miller, and M. C. Hammer.
Jobete Music Co., Inc., 1990/Stone City Music, 1990/Stone Diamond
   Music Corp., 1990/Bust It Publishing, 1990.
Best-selling record by M. C. Hammer from *Please Hammer Don't Hurt
   'Em* (Capitol, 90). Based on the 1981 Rick James classic "Super
   Freak." Won a Grammy Award for Best Rhythm & Blues Song of
   the Year. Nominated for a Grammy Award for Best Record of the
   Year.

Unanswered Prayers
Words and music by Pat Alger, Larry Bastain, and Garth Brooks.
Bait and Beer, 1990/Forerunner/Midsummer Music/Major Bob
   Music.
Best-selling record by Garth Brooks from *No Fences* (Capitol, 90).

Unbelievable (English)
Words and music by Yello.
TCF, 1990.
Introduced by Yello in the film and on the soundtrack album *Ford
   Fairlane* (Elektra, 90).

Unchained Melody
Revived by The Righteous Brothers from *The Righteous Brothers
   Greatest Hits* (Verve/Polydor, 89) and in the film and its soundtrack
   album *Ghost* (Curb, 90). For copyright information see *Popular
   Music 1920-1979*.

Under My Thumb (English)
Revived by Sam Kinison on *Leader of the Banned* (Warner Bros., 90).
   Rolling Stones hit spoofed by the high-strung comedian. For
   copyright information, see *Popular Music, 1920-1979*.

Under the Gun
Words and music by Randy Newman.
Introduced by Randy Newman as the theme to the TV musical drama *Cop Rock* (90).

Under the Sea
Revived by Buster Poindexter (RCA, 90). For copyright information see *Popular Music, 1989.* The original version by Sam Wright was nominated for a Grammy Award for Best Song for TV or Film. Nominated for a Grammy Award, Song for TV or Film, 1990.

Unlikely Lovers
Words and music by William Finn.
Introduced by Michael Rupert, Stephen Bogardes, Heather MacRae, and Janet Metz in the play *Return to Falsettoland* (90).

Unskinny Bop
Words and music by Bobby Dall, C. C. Deville, Bret Michaels, and Rikki Rockett.
Sweet Cyanide, 1990/Willesden Music, Inc.
Best-selling record by Poison from *Flesh and Blood* (Capitol, 90).

Until You Come Back To Me
Revived by Miki Howard from *Miki Howard* (Atlantic, 89). For copyright information see *Popular Music 1920-1979.*

V

Vision of Love
Words and music by Mariah Carey and Ben Margulies.
Vision of Love Songs Inc., 1990/Been Jammin'.
Best-selling record by Mariah Carey from *Mariah Carey* (Columbia, 90). One of the year's biggest ballads, sung by the year's biggest voice. Nominated for Grammy awards for Best Song of the Year and Best Record of the Year.

Vogue
Words and music by Madonna Ciccone and Shep Pettibone.
WB Music Corp., 1989/Bleu Disque Music/Webo Girl Music/WB Music Corp./Lexor.
Best-selling record by Madonna from *Like a Prayer* (Warner Bros., 89). Ushering in a new dance craze.

W

Walk on
Words and music by Steve Dean and Lonnie Williams.
Tom Collins Music Corp., 1988.
Best-selling record by Reba McEntire from *Reba Live* (MCA, 89).

Walk on By
Revived by Sybil from *Sybil* (Next Plateau, 89). For copyright information see *Popular Music 1920-1979*.

Walk on the Wild Side
Revived by Edie Brickell & New Bohemians in the film and on the soundtrack album *Flashback* (WTB, 90). For copyright information see *Popular Music, 1920-1979*.

Walk with the Night (Scottish)
Words by Jimmie O'Neill.
Introduced by The Silencers on *A Blues for Buddah* (RCA, 89).

Walkin' Away
Words and music by Clint Black, Hayden Nicholas, and Dick Gay.
Howlin' Hits Music, 1989.
Best-selling record by Clint Black from *Killin' Time* (RCA, 89).

Walking Shoes
Words and music by Paul Kennerley.
Irving Music Inc., 1990/Little March.
Best-selling record by Tanya Tucker from *Tennessee Woman* (Capitol, 90).

Wanted
Words and music by Alan Jackson and Charlie Craig.
Mattie Ruth, 1990/Seventh Son/EMI-Blackwood Music Inc.
Best-selling record by Alan Jackson from *Here in the Real World* (Arista, 90).

The Way You Do the Things You Do
Revived by UB40 from *Labour of Love II* (Virgin, 90). For copyright information see *Popular Music 1920-1979*.

We Belong Together
Words by Ken Wydro and Vi Higgensen, music by Wesley Naylor.
Reach Songs, 1990.
Performed by D'atra Higgins and Norwood in the musical and on the original cast album of *Mama, I Want to Sing II* (Reach, 90).

We Can't Go Wrong
Words and music by Andy Tripoli, Tony Moran, and Gardner Cole.
Andy Panda, 1989/Zomba Enterprises, Inc./Latin Rascals/Red Instructional Music/Disco Fever Publishing/Salski.
Best-selling record by The Cover Girls from *We Can't Go Wrong* (Capitol, 89).

We Gotta Get Out of This Place
Rhythm 'n' Blues Katrina & The Waves on the TV series *China Beach* and on its soundtrack album (SBK, 90). For copyright information, see *Popular Music 1920-1979*.

The Weeping Song (English)
Words and music by Nick Cave.
Dying Art, 1990.
Introduced by Nick Cave & the Bad Seeds on *The Good Son* (Elektra, 90).

Welcome to the Terrordome
Words and music by Hank Shocklee, Keith Shocklee, and Carlton Ridenhour.
Def American Songs, 1989.
Best-selling record by Public Enemy from *Fear of a Black Planet* (Def Jam, 90).

What Can You Lose
Words and music by Stephen Sondheim.
Rilting Music Inc., 1990/WB Music Corp.
Introduced by Madonna in the film *Dick Tracy* and on her LP *I'm Breathless* (Sire, 90).

What Goes Around
Words and music by Carolyn Mitchell.
Reata Publishing Inc., 1989/Peach Pie/Tunes-R-Us/KMA Tunes.
Best-selling record by Regina Belle from *Stay with Me* (Columbia, 89).

What It Takes
Words and music by Steven Tyler, Joe Perry, and Desmond Child.

Swag Song Music, 1989/Desmobile Music Co./EMI-April Music Inc.
Best-selling record by Aerosmith from *Pump* (Geffen, 89).

What Kind of Man Would I Be?
Words and music by Jason Scheff, Charles Sandford, and Bobby
    Caldwell.
Texas City, 1989/Jason Scheff/EMI-Blackwood Music
    Inc./Sindrome/Fallwater Music.
Best-selling record Chicago from *Greatest Hits 1982-1989* (Reprise, 89).

What More Can I Say
Words and music by William Finn.
Introduced in the musical *Return to Falsettoland* by Michael Rupert.

When Do the Bells Ring for Me
Words and music by Charles DeForest.
Charles DeForest Music Publishing Co., 1990/Benedetto Music.
Introduced by Tony Bennett on *Astoria: Portrait of an Artist*
    (Columbia, 90).

When I Call Your Name
Words and music by Vince Gill and Tim Dubois.
Benefit, 1990/WB Music Corp.
Best-selling record by Vince Gill from *When I Call Your Name* (MCA,
    90). Nominated for a Grammy Award for Country Song of the Year.

When I'm Back on My Feet Again
Words and music by Diane Warren.
Realsongs, 1989.
Best-selling record by Michael Bolton from *Soul Provider* (Columbia,
    89).

When the Lights Go Out
Words and music by Bruce Springsteen.
Bruce Springsteen Publishing, 1990.
Introduced by Bruce Springsteen at a benefit in Los Angeles.

When You Got a Good Friend
Words and music by Robert Johnson.
King of Spades Music, 1990.
Revived by Robert Johnson on *The Complete Recordings* (Columbia,
    90).

Where Do We Go from Here
Words and music by LeMel Humes.

Virgin Songs, 1989/Buffalo Music Factory.
Best-selling record by Stacy Lattisaw with Johnny Gill from *What You Need* (Motown, 89).

Where Do You Go from Love
Words and music by Charles DeForest.
Charles DeForest Music Publishing Co./Benedetto Music.
Introduced by Tony Bennett on *Astoria: Portrait of an Artist* (Columbia, 90).

Where've You Been
Words and music by Don Henry and Jon Vezner.
Cross Keys Publishing Co., Inc., 1988/Wrensong.
Best-selling record by Kathy Mattea from *Willow in the Wind* (Polygram, 89). Won a Grammy Award for Best Country Song of the Year. Winner of a Country Music Association award for Best Country Song of the Year. Vezner is Mattea's husband.

Whip Appeal
Words and music by Babyface (pseudonym for Kenny Edmunds) and Pete Q. Smith.
Epic/Solar, 1989/Kear Music/Jenn-a-Bug Music.
Best-selling record by Babyface from *Tender Love* (Epic, 89).

Whistling in the Dark
Words and music by They Might Be Giants.
They Might Be Giants Music, 1989.
Introduced by They Might Be Giants on *Flood* (Elektra, 90).

White Line
Words and music by Neil Young.
Silver Fiddle, 1990.
Introduced by Neil Young & Crazy Horse on *Ragged Glory* (Reprise, 90).

Who Stole the Soul
Words and music by Chuck D (pseudonym for Charles Ridenhour).
Def American Songs, 1990/Your Mother's.
Introduced by Public Enemy on *Fear of a Black Planet* (Def Jam/Columbia, 90).

Whole Wide World (from *True Love*)
Words and music by Elliott Wolff and Arnie Roman.
Virgin Music, Inc., 1989/Elliott Wolff Music/Jobete Music Co., Inc.
Best-selling record by A'me Lorain from the film and soundtrack album *True Love* (RCA, 90).

Why You Get Funky on Me (from *House Party*)
Words and music by William Aquart and Gene Griffen.
Virgin Songs, 1990/Cal-Gene Music.
Best-selling record by Today from *House Party* film and soundtrack (Motown, 90).

Wicked Game
Words and music by Chris Isaak.
Chris Isaak Music Publishing, 1989.
Performed by Chris Isaak in the film and the soundtrack LP *Wild at Heart*. Introduced on *Heart-shaped World* (Warner Bros., 89).

Wiggle It
Words and music by George Morel and R. Vargas.
Cutting Music, 1990/Groove/Dose Rocks.
Best-selling record by 2 in a Room from *Wiggle It* (Cutting Records, 90).

The Wish
Words and music by Bruce Springsteen.
Bruce Springsteen Publishing, 1990.
Introduced by Bruce Springsteen in concert at L.A.'s Shrine Auditorium on a bill with Bonnie Raitt and Jackson Browne.

With These Hands
Words and music by Abner Silver and Benny Davis.
TRO-Cromwell Music Inc., 1990.
Introduced by Tom Jones in the film and on the soundtrack to *Edward Scissorhands* (MCA, 90).

Without You
Words and music by Nikki Sixx and Mick Mars.
Motley Crue, 1989/Sikki Nixx/Mick Mars.
Best-selling record by Motley Crue from *Dr. Feelgood* (Elektra, 89).

Woman in the Wall (English)
Words and music by Paul Heaton and David Rotheray.
Go! Discs Ltd., England, 1989.
Introduced by The Beautiful South on *Welcome to the Beautiful South* (Elektra, 90).

Work
Words and music by Lou Reed and John Cale.
Metal Machine Music, 1989/John Cale.
Introduced by Lou Reed and John Cale on *Songs for Drella* (Sire, 90).

Wow

Words and music by Gerome Ragni, James Rado, and Galt
MacDermot.

Introduced by James Rado, Gerome Ragni, and Galt MacDermot in a
special cabaret performance of songs from their projected musical,
Sun.

Y

You Can't Bring Me Down
Words and music by Mike Muir and Rocky George.
You'll Be Sorry, 1990.
Introduced by Suicidal Tendencies on *Lights...Camera...Revolution* (Epic, 90).

You Can't Deny It (English)
Words and music by Lisa Stansfield, Ian Devaney, and Andy Morris.
Big Life, 1990.
Best-selling record by Lisa Stansfield from *Affection* (Arista, 90).

You Lie
Words and music by Bobby Fisher, Austin Roberts, and Charlie Black.
Bobby Fisher, 1990/Five Bar-B/Chriswald Music/Hopi Sound Music/Krismik.
Best-selling record by Reba McEntire on *Rumor Has It* (MCA, 90).

You Really Had Me Going
Words and music by Tom Shapiro and Chris Waters.
Careers Music Inc., 1990/Edge O'Woods/Moline Valley/Kinetic Diamond.
Best-selling record by Holly Dunn from *Heart Full of Love* (Warner Bros., 90).

You Win Again
Words and music by Mary Chapin Carpenter.
EMI-April Music Inc., 1990/Getarealjob Music.
Introduced by Mary Chapin Carpenter on *Shooting Straight in the Dark* (Columbia, 90).

Your Baby Never Looked Good in Blue
Words and music by Diane Warren.

Realsongs, 1989/Pax Music.
Best-selling record by Expose from *What You Don't Know* (Arista, 89).
Capping off a banner year for songwriter Warren.

You're the One
Words and music by Steve Ferguson.
WB Music Corp., 1977/The Ferguson.
Performed by The Carpenters on the TV movie *The Karen Carpenter Story* and on the album *Love Lines* (A&M, 89).

Yuppies in the Sky
Words and music by Tom Paxton.
Pax Music, 1985.
Revived by Peter, Paul & Mary on *Flowers and Stones* (Gold Castle, 90). A final word on an '80s phenomenon, better late than never.

Lyricists & Composers Index

Lyricists & Composers Index

Lyricists & Composers Index

Lyricists & Composers Index

Lyricists & Composers Index

Lyricists & Composers Index

Lyricists & Composers Index

Lyricists & Composers Index

Important Performances Index

Songs are listed under the works in which they were introduced or given significant renditions. The index is organized into major sections by performance medium: Album, Movie, Musical, Performer, Revue, Television Show.

Awards Index

A list of songs nominated for Academy Awards by the Academy of Motion Picture Arts and Sciences and Grammy Awards from the National Academy of Recording Arts and Sciences. Asterisks indicate the winners.

1990

Academy Award
  Blaze of Glory (from *Young Guns II*)
  I'm Checking Out
  Promise Me You'll Remember (Love Theme from *The Godfather III*)
  Somewhere in My Memory
  Sooner or Later (I Always Get My Man)*
Grammy Award
  Alright
  Another Day in Paradise
  Another Day in Paradise*
  Blaze of Glory (from *Young Guns II*)
  Come Next Monday
  The Dance
  Friends in Low Places
  From a Distance*
  From a Distance
  Here and Now
  Hold On
  I'll Be Good to You
  Kiss the Girl
  More
  My, My, My
  Nothing Compares 2 U
  Sooner or Later (I Always Get My Man)
  U Can't Touch This
  U Can't Touch This*
  Under the Sea
  Vision of Love
  When I Call Your Name
  Where've You Been*

List of Publishers

A directory of publishers of the songs included in *Popular Music,* 1990. Publishers that are members of the American Society of Composers, Authors, and Publishers or whose catalogs are available under ASCAP license are indicated by the designation (ASCAP). Publishers that have granted performing rights to Broadcast Music, Inc., are designated by the notation (BMI). Publishers whose catalogs are represented by SESAC, Inc., are indicated by the designation (SESAC).

The addresses were gleaned from a variety of sources, including ASCAP, BMI, SESAC, *Billboard* magazine, and the National Music Publishers' Association. As in any volatile industry, many of the addresses may become outdated quickly. In the interim between the book's completion and its subsequent publication, some publishers may have been consolidated into others or changed hands. This is a fact of life long endured by the music business and its constituents. The data collected here, and throughout the book, are as accurate as such circumstances allow. Where only the publisher's name is listed, addresses were not available.

A

ABKCO Music Inc. (BMI)
    1700 Broadway
    New York, New York 10019

Across 110th Street (ASCAP)
    c/o SBK Songs
    1290 Avenue of the Americas
    New York, New York 10019

Aerostation Corp. (ASCAP)
    16214 Morrison Street
    Encino, California 91436

AGF Music Ltd. (ASCAP)
    1500 Broadway, Suite 2805
    New York, New York 10036

Aixoise Music (ASCAP)
    see Lost Lake Arts Music

Albedo (ASCAP)
    1365 Dunning Dr.
    Laguna Beach, California 92651

Alley Music (BMI)
    1619 Broadway, 11th Fl.
    New York, New York 10019

Almo Music Corp. (ASCAP)
    1416 N. La Brea Avenue
    Hollywood, California 90028

AlshaMighty

Amanda-Lin

List of Publishers

Andite Invasion (BMI)
c/o Hal Bynum
430 Third Avenue, N.
Nashville, Tennessee 37201

Andy Panda (ASCAP)
see Zomba Enterprises, Inc.

Anlon Music Co. (ASCAP)
see Cherry Lane Music Co., Inc.

Another Stronger Song

Aresville (BMI)
8502 Village Green Dr.
Cross Plains, Tennessee 37049

Arista Music, Inc.
8370 Wilshire Blvd.
Beverly Hills, California 90211

Audre Mae Music (BMI)
34 Dogwood Drive
Smithtown, New York 11787

B

Bait and Beer (ASCAP)
c/o Terrell Tye
P.O. Box 120657
Nashville, Tennessee 37212

Baledat (BMI)
see Willesden Music, Inc.

Bamatuck (ASCAP)
21 Music Square East
Nashville, Tennessee 37203

Basically Gasp Music (ASCAP)
115 Ivy Drive, No. 10
Charlottesville, Virginia 22901

Bay (BMI)
see EMI-Blackwood Music Inc.

Beechwood Music Corp. (BMI)
6255 Sunset Blvd.
Hollywood, California 90028

Been Jammin' (BMI)
c/o J. Greco
63 St. Marks Pl., #4B
New York City, New York 10003

Beeswing Music (BMI)
c/o Gary Stamler
2029 Century Park, E., Suite 1500
Los Angeles, California 90067

Benedetto Music (ASCAP)
101 W. 55th St.
New York City, New York 10019

Benefit (BMI)

John Bettis Music (ASCAP)
c/o Harley Williams
1900 Avenue of the Stars
Suite 1200
Los Angeles, California 90067

Beyerson (BMI)

Big Life

Big Thrilling Music (ASCAP)
see Of the Fire Music

Black Chick (ASCAP)
see Almo Music Corp.

Black Ice Music (BMI)
see Flyte Tyme Tunes

Black Lion (ASCAP)
6525 Sunset Blvd., 2nd Fl.
Hollywood, California 90028

Bleu Disque Music (ASCAP)
c/o Warner Brothers Music
9000 Sunset Blvd., Penthouse
Los Angeles, California 90069

Block & Gilbert (ASCAP)
see BMG Music

Blue Gator Music (ASCAP)
c/o Bernard Gudvit Co. Inc.
6420 Wilshire Blvd., Suite 425
Los Angeles, California 90048

Blue Sky Rider Songs (BMI)
c/o Prager and Fenton
6363 Sunset Blvd., Suite 706
Los Angeles, California 90028

Bluebear Waltzes

Blues Palace (ASCAP)
539 Atlantic St.
Bethlehem, Pennsylvania 18015

Blues Traveler

BMC (ASCAP)

BMG Music (ASCAP)
1133 Sixth Avenue
New York, New York 10036

Bob-a-Lew Songs (ASCAP)
P.O. Box 8031
Universal City, California 91608

Bocephus Music Inc. (BMI)
see Singletree Music Co., Inc.

Bogam (ASCAP)

Bon Jovi Publishing (ASCAP)
c/o Siegel & Feldstein
509 Madison Avenue
New York, New York 10022

Bona Relations Music (BMI)
see WB Music Corp.

Boneidol Music (ASCAP)
c/o Aucoin Management Inc.
645 Madison Avenue
New York, New York 10022

Alain Boublil Music Inc. (ASCAP)
1776 Broadway
New York, New York 10019

Broadhead (BMI)

Brontosaurus (ASCAP)
14543 Burbank Blvd, #116
Van Nuys, California 91411

Bobby Brown (ASCAP)
see EMI-April Music Inc.

Buff Man

Buffalo Music Factory (BMI)

Bug Music (BMI)
Bug Music Group
6777 Hollywood Blvd., 9th Fl.
Hollywood, California 90028

Burning Publishing Co. Ltd.

Bust It Publishing (BMI)
c/o Manatt Phelps and Phillips
11355 W. Olympic Blvd.
Los Angeles, California 90064

Bill Butler Music (BMI)
1703 19th Street
Hondo, Texas 78861

C

Cal-Gene Music (BMI)
c/o Sound of New York Records
230 W. 230th Street, No. 1450
Bronx, New York 10463

John Cale (BMI)
c/o Chrisopher Whent Esq.
270 Madison Ave., Ste. 1410
New York City, New York 10016

California Phase Music (ASCAP)
c/o Fitzgerald Hartley Co.
7250 Beverly Blvd., Suite 200
Los Angeles, California 90036

Calloco
Address Unavailable

Buddy Cannon Music (ASCAP)
Route 202, Box 403
Kingston Springs, Tennessee 37082

Careers Music Inc. (ASCAP)
see Arista Music, Inc.

Carlooney Tunes (ASCAP)
see Chrysalis Music Corp.

Carmit

Cass County Music Co. (ASCAP)
c/o Breslauer, Jacobson & Rutman
10880 Wilshire Blvd., Suite 2110
Los Angeles, California 90024

Ceros (BMI)
see Bug Music

C'est Music (ASCAP)
see Quackenbush Music, Ltd.

Joe Chambers (ASCAP)
see Tree Publishing Co., Inc.

List of Publishers

Chappell & Co., Inc. (ASCAP)
810 Seventh Avenue
New York, New York 10019

Deena Charles

Chelcait Music (BMI)
6124 Selma Avenue
Hollywood, California 90028

Cherry Lane Music Co., Inc. (ASCAP)
110 Midland Avenue
Port Chester, New York 10573

Chi-Boy (ASCAP)
c/o Schwartz & Farquharson
9107 Wilshire Blvd., Suite 300
Beverly Hills, California 90216

Chicago Brothers Music (BMI)
3612 Barnham Blvd.
Los Angeles, California 90028

Christian Burial Music (ASCAP)
c/o The New York End Ltd.
143 W. 69th Street, Suite 2A
New York, New York 10023

Chriswald Music (ASCAP)
6255 Sunset Blvd., Suite 1911
Hollywood, California 90028

Chrysalis Music Corp. (ASCAP)
Chrysalis Music Group
645 Madison Avenue
New York, New York 10022

Clairaudient (BMI)

Coal Dust West (BMI)
c/o Zifrin, Brittenham & Branca
2121 Avenue of the Stars
Los Angeles, California 90067

Coburn (BMI)
see Bug Music

Cold Chillin' (ASCAP)
see WB Music Corp.

Coleision (BMI)
see EMI-Blackwood Music Inc.

Colgems-EMI Music Inc. (ASCAP)
see Screen Gems-EMI Music Inc.

Collins Court Music, Inc. (ASCAP)
P.O. Box 121407
Nashville, Tennessee 37212

Tom Collins Music Corp. (BMI)
P.O. Box 121407
Nashville, Tennessee 37212

Companion

Consenting Adult (BMI)
see Screen Gems-EMI Music Inc.

Controversy Music (ASCAP)
c/o Manatt, Phelps, Rothenberg
Att: Lee Phillips
11355 W. Olympic Blvd.
Los Angeles, California 90064

Coolwell Music (ASCAP)
c/o Granite Music Corp.
6124 Selma Avenue
Los Angeles, California 90028

Copyright Control (ASCAP)
see Bug Music

Copyright Management

Crab Salad Music (BMI)
see Virgin Music, Inc.

CRGI (BMI)
c/o CBS (Sony Records)
666 5th Ave.
New York City, New York 10103

Cross Keys Publishing Co., Inc. (ASCAP)
see Tree Publishing Co., Inc.

Cutting Music (ASCAP)
111 Dyckman Street
New York, New York 10040

D

Bobby D (ASCAP)
see WB Music Corp.

Dare to Dream Music (ASCAP)
483 Empire Blvd.
Brooklyn, New York 11225

Davince Music (ASCAP)
c/o Bug Music Group
6777 Hollywood Blvd., 9th Fl.
Hollywood, California 90028

Daywin Music, Inc. (BMI)
c/o Six Continents Music
Publishing, Inc.
8304 Beverly Blvd.
Los Angeles, California 90048

Dead Los Angeles (BMI)
see I.R.S.

Dee Klein (BMI)
see Almo Music Corp.

Def American Songs (BMI)
298 Elizabeth Street
New York, New York 10012

Charles DeForest Music Publishing Co.
(ASCAP)
309 W. 57th St.
New York City, New York 10019

Delovely (ASCAP)
see Zomba Enterprises, Inc.

De'Mar

Twyla Dent Music (ASCAP)

Desmobile Music Co. (ASCAP)
Att: Desmond Child
12 W. 72nd Street
New York, New York 10023

Devo Music (BMI)
c/o Unichappel Music Inc.
810 Seventh Avenue
New York, New York 10019

Diabetic (ASCAP)
637 W. 103rd St.
Los Angeles, California 90044

Difficult Music (BMI)
c/o Beldock, Levine & Hoffman
565 Fifth Avenue
New York, New York 10017

Donna Dijon

Disco Fever Publishing (ASCAP)
P.O. Box 219
Yonkers, New York 10710

Doc Ice (BMI)
see Island Music

Doraflo (BMI)

Doraflo Music, Inc. (BMI)
c/o Al Kohn
Warner Brothers Music
9200 Sunset Blvd., Suite 222
Los Angeles, California 90069

Dose Rocks (ASCAP)
701 W. 176th St., #4F
New York, New York 10033

Double Exposure Music Inc. (ASCAP)
see WB Music Corp.

Dick Dragon Music (BMI)
see Virgin Music, Inc.

Duke of Earle (ASCAP)
c/o Side One Management
1775 Broadway, 7th Fl.
New York, New York 10019

Duncanne Hille (BMI)
8707 Westknoll Dr.
Los Angeles, California 90069

Dying Art

E

E/A (BMI)
c/o Warner-Tamerlane
9000 Sunset Blvd.
Los Angeles, California 90069

Barry Eastmond Music (ASCAP)
400 E. 17th Street
New York, New York 11226

Eberhardt Music (ASCAP)

Eden Music, Inc. (BMI)
P.O. Box 325
Englewood, New Jersey 07631

Edge O'Woods (ASCAP)
1214 16th Ave. South
Nashville, Tennessee 37212

Edisto Sound Int'l (BMI)
see CRGI

List of Publishers

EEG Music (ASCAP)
see Chappell & Co., Inc.

E.G. Music, Inc. (BMI)
161 W. 54th Street
New York, New York 10019

Egypt Hollow (BMI)
c/o Copyright Management Inc.
1102 7th Ave. S., Ste. 400
Nashville, Tennessee 37212

EMI April Canada

EMI-April Music Inc. (ASCAP)
49 E. 52nd Street
New York, New York 10022

EMI-Blackwood Music Inc. (BMI)
1350 Avenue of the Americas
23rd Fl.
New York, New York 10019

EMI Songs Ltd.

Emile Music
509 Madison Avenue, Suite 1810
New York, New York 10022

End of August (ASCAP)
see Tree Publishing Co., Inc.

Ensign Music Corp. (BMI)
c/o Sidney Herman
1 Gulf & Western Plaza
New York, New York 10023

Epic/Solar (BMI)
see Kear Music

ESP Management Inc. (BMI)
Att: E. S. Prager
1790 Broadway
New York, New York 10019

Esta Chica (BMI)

Evil Eye Music Inc. (BMI)
see Songways Service Inc.

F

Fallwater Music (BMI)
see Hudson Bay Music Co.

Famous Monster (BMI)
140 E. Seventh Street
New York, New York 10009

Famous Music Corp. (ASCAP)
Gulf & Western Industries, Inc.
1 Gulf & Western Plaza
New York, New York 10023

Fee Music

Fellow (BMI)
see Intersong, USA Inc.

The Ferguson (ASCAP)
see WB Music Corp.

Fiction Music Inc. (BMI)
P.O. Box 135
Bearsville, New York 12409

Fiddleback Music Publishing Co., Inc. (BMI)
1270 Avenue of the Americas
New York, New York 10020

Figaro Music (BMI)
12257 Landale St.
Studio City, California 91604

Bobby Fisher (ASCAP)
1618 16th Ave. South
Nashville, Tennessee 37212

Five Bar-B

Stephen Flaherty
see WB Music Corp.

Fleedleedee Music (ASCAP)
c/o Jess Morgan & Co.
6420 Wilshire Blvd.
Los Angeles, California 90048

Flip a Jig (ASCAP)
Address Unavailable

Danny Flowers (BMI)
Address Unavailable

Flyte Tyme Tunes (ASCAP)
c/o Avant Garde Music Publishing
9229 Sunset Blvd., Suite 311
Los Angeles, California 90069

For Our Children (ASCAP)
see Zomba Enterprises, Inc.

Forceful Music (BMI)
c/o Williston Music
P.O. Box 284
Brooklyn, New York 11203

Foreign Imported (BMI)
8921 S.W. Tenth Terrace
Miami, Florida 33174

Forerunner (ASCAP)
P.O. Box 120657
Nashville, Tennessee 37212

Forever

Fox Film Music Corp. (BMI)
c/o Twentieth Century Fox Film Corp
P.O. Box 900
Beverly Hills, California 90213

Frank Music Co. (ASCAP)
see MPL Communications Inc.

Freedom (BMI)

J. French Music

Frisco Kid Music (ASCAP)
c/o Cooper, Epstein, Hurewitz
9465 Wilshire Blvd., No. 800
Beverly Hills, California 90212

Fuju Pacific Music, Inc.

Full Keel (ASCAP)
4450 Lakeside Dr., Ste. 200
Burbank, California 91505

Funzalo Music (BMI)
225 W. 57th Street
New York, New York 10019

G

Gabeson (BMI)
c/o Meitus Copyright
2851 Laurana Road
Union, New Jersey 07083

Ganga Publishing Co. (BMI)
see Screen Gems-EMI Music Inc.

Garden Court Music Co. (ASCAP)
45 Holton Avenue
Montreal, Quebec H3Y 2G1
Canada

Geffen Music (ASCAP)
c/o Warner Bros. Music
9000 Sunset Blvd.
Los Angeles, California 90069

Getarealjob Music (ASCAP)
c/o Studio One Artists
P.O. Box 5824
Bethesda, Maryland 20814

GLG Two (BMI)
13624 Sherman Way, #450
Van Nuys, California 91405

Godhap Music (BMI)
see Virgin Music, Inc.

Gold Forever Music Inc. (BMI)
see EMI-Blackwood Music Inc.

Golden Mountain Music Inc. (ASCAP)
c/o Freedman Snow & Co.
1092 Mount Pleasant Road
Toronto, Ontario M4P 2M6
Canada

Golden Torch Music Corp. (ASCAP)
c/o Columbia Pictures
Att: Lee Reed
Columbia Plaza
Burbank, California 91505

Goldline Music Inc. (ASCAP)
see Silverline Music, Inc.

Gomace Music, Inc. (BMI)
1000 N. Doheny Drive
Los Angeles, California 90069

Gone Gator Music (ASCAP)
c/o Bernard Gudvi & Co., Inc.
6420 Wilshire Blvd., Suite 425
Los Angeles, California 90048

Gracie Films (BMI)

Granary Music (BMI)
c/o Linda Clark
P.O. Box 1304
Burbank, California 91507

Grass Root Productions (BMI)
c/o Arthur T. Lee
4717 Don Lorenzo Drive
Los Angeles, California 90008

List of Publishers

Great Lips Music (BMI)
see Virgin Music, Inc.

Green Skirt Music (BMI)
see Kear Music

Groove

Guns N' Roses Music (ASCAP)
see Cherry Lane Music Co., Inc.

Gunster (ASCAP)
see EMI-April Music Inc.

H

Hallenbeck Music Co. (BMI)
c/o Greene & Reynolds
Att: Bob Greene
1900 Avenue of the Stars
Suite 1424
Los Angeles, California 90067

Albert Hammond (ASCAP)
Address Unavailable

Hamstein Music (BMI)
c/o Bill Ham
P.O. Box 19647
Houston, Texas 77024

Hancock Music Co. (BMI)
c/o David Rubinson & Friends Inc.
827 Folsom Street
San Francisco, California 94107

Hannah's Eyes (BMI)
1116 Frances Ave.
Nashville, Tennessee 371204

Hayes Street (ASCAP)
see Almo Music Corp.

Haynestorm Music (ASCAP)
c/o William A. Coben, Esq.
2029 Century Park, E.
Suite 1700
Los Angeles, California 90067

He Dog (ASCAP)

Head Cheese (ASCAP)
see PRI Music

Heart Street (ASCAP)
14300 TerraBelle St. #44
Panorama City, California 91402

Hee Bee Dooinit (ASCAP)
see WB Music Corp.

Hereford (ASCAP)
6400 Hollis, Ste. 8
Emeryville, California 94608

Hi-Frost

Hidden Pun (BMI)
1841 Broadway
New York, New York 10023

Hillsdale Music
see WB Music Corp.

Hip-Trip Music Co. (BMI)
c/o Glen E. Davis
1635 N. Cahuenga Blvd., 6th Fl.
Hollywood, California 90028

Hit & Run Music (ASCAP)
1841 Broadway, Suite 411
New York, New York 10023

Hittage (ASCAP)
16 W. 22nd St.
New York City, New York 10010

Holmes Line of Music (ASCAP)
228 W. 71st Street
New York, New York 10023

Homeland

Hoochie Coochie (BMI)
see Bug Music

Hook 'N B (ASCAP)
see CBS Songs Ltd.

Hopi Sound Music (ASCAP)
c/o Chris De Walden
6255 Sunset Blvd., Suite 1911
Hollywood, California 90028

Hori Productions America Inc. (ASCAP)
410 Park Ave.
New York, New York 10022

Hot Cha Music Co. (BMI)
see Six Continents Music Publishing Inc.

Hot Toddy Music

House of Fun Music (BMI)
c/o John Benitez
1775 Broadway
New York, New York 10019

House Projects (ASCAP)
see CBS Songs Ltd.

Howlin' Hits Music (ASCAP)
P.O. Box 19647
Houston, Texas 77224

Hudson Bay Music Co. (BMI)
1619 Broadway, Suite 906
New York, New York 10019

I

Ice Age Music (ASCAP)
c/o Segel & Goldman
9348 Santa Monica Blvd.
Beverly Hills, California 90210

Ice Baby

International Velvet (BMI)
see Bug Music

Intersong, USA Inc.
c/o Chappell & Co., Inc.
810 Seventh Avenue
New York, New York 10019

I.R.S. (BMI)
Address Unavailable

Irving Music Inc. (BMI)
1358 N. La Brea
Hollywood, California 90028

Is Hot Music, Ltd. (ASCAP)
34 Pheasant Run
Old Westbury, New York 11568

Chris Isaak Music Publishing (ASCAP)
P.O. Box 547
Larkspur, California 94939

Island Music (BMI)
c/o Mr. Lionel Conway
6525 Sunset Blvd.
Hollywood, California 90028

Itsall (BMI)
see Irving Music Inc.

Itself and Macdaddi (ASCAP)
see Haynestorm Music

J

Jenn-a-Bug Music (ASCAP)
c/o Manatt, Phelps, Rothenberg
11355 W. Olympic Blvd.
Los Angeles, California 90064

Jesse Boy (ASCAP)
see Virgin Music, Inc.

Jesse Jo (BMI)

Jig-a-Watt Jams (BMI)
Division of New Day Publishing Co.
1948 Fullerton Drive
Cincinnati, Ohio 45240

Jo Skin (ASCAP)
see Zomba Enterprises, Inc.

Jobete Music Co., Inc. (ASCAP)
Att: Erlinda N. Barrios
6255 Sunset Blvd., Suite 1600
Hollywood, California 90028

Joel (BMI)
c/o Maritime Music Inc.
200 W. 57th Street
New York, New York 10019

Jones Music Co.
c/o Dorothy Mae Rice Jones
1916 Portman Avenue
Cincinnati, Ohio 45237

K

K-Mark (ASCAP)
see EMI-April Music Inc.

Kear Music (BMI)
Division of La Face, Inc.
c/o Carter Turner & Co.
9229 Sunset Blvd.
Los Angeles, California 90069

Kidada Music Inc. (BMI)
7250 Beverly Blvd., Suite 206
Los Angeles, California 90036

List of Publishers

Kikinit (BMI)
see EMI-Blackwood Music Inc.

Kinetic Diamond (ASCAP)
513 Hill Road
Nashville, Tennessee 37220

King of Spades Music

Stephen A. Kipner Music (ASCAP)
Att: Stephen A. Kipner
19646 Valley View Drive
Topanga, California 90290

Kitchen Music (BMI)
see EMI-Blackwood Music Inc.

Kittus Corp. (ASCAP)
230 Park Ave., Ste. 915
New York, New York 10169

KMA Tunes (ASCAP)
196 E. Boston Post Road
Mamaroneck, New York 10543

Knighty Knight (ASCAP)
see Arista Music, Inc.

Kortchmar Music (ASCAP)
c/o Nick M. Ben-Meir
644 N. Doheny Drive
Los Angeles, California 90069

Krismik (ASCAP)
6255 Sunset Blvd, Ste. 915
Hollywood, California 90028

L

La Rana (BMI)
1750 E. Holly Avenue
El Segundo, California 90245

Lake of the Pine

Lake Victoria Music (ASCAP)
c/o Stephen H. Cooper, Esq.
Weil, Gotschal & Manges
767 Fifth Avenue
New York, New York 10022

Lambardoni Edizioni (ASCAP)
see Intersong, USA Inc.

Lamek Pub. (BMI)
5775 N. Crestwood Blvd.
Milwaukee, Wisconsin 53209

Al Lancellotti (ASCAP)
see EMI-April Music Inc.

Larrikin Music

Latin Rascals (BMI)
c/o Tin Pan Apple Inc.
250 W. 57th St., Ste. 1723
New York City, New York 10107

Laughing Dogs (BMI)

Lorna Lee (BMI)
c/o CBS Music Pub.
Attn: H. Condra
Eight Music Square W.
P.O. Box 1273
Nashville, Tennessee 37202

Oliver Leiber Music (ASCAP)
see Virgin Music, Inc.

Leo Sun

Les Etoiles de la Musique (ASCAP)
c/o William A. Coben, Esq.
2029 Century Park, E., Suite 2600
Los Angeles, California 90067

Level Vibes (ASCAP)

Lexor (ASCAP)
see Zomba Enterprises, Inc.

Liafail (BMI)

Likete Split Music (BMI)
see Lake Victoria Music

Lillybilly
see Bug Music

Linde Manor Publishing Co. (BMI)
Rte. 1, Lakeview Dr.
Hermitage, Tennessee 37076

Little Diva Music (BMI)
2029 Centry Park
Los Angeles, California 90067

Little March (BMI)
see Irving Music Inc.

Little Reata (BMI)
see Irving Music Inc.

Liu Tunes
9102 Seventeenth NE
Seattle, Washington 98115

Long Pond Music
see Revelation Music Publishing Corp.

Longitude Music (BMI)
c/o Windswept Pacific Entertainment Co.
4450 Lakeside Drive, Suite 200
Burbank, California 91505

Lost Lake Arts Music (ASCAP)
Division of Windham Hill Production s, Inc.
831 High Street
Palo Alto, California 94301

Louie Louie Entertainment (ASCAP)
509 East Street Gertrude
Santa Ana, California 92707

Low Key (BMI)
see Willesden Music, Inc.

Lucrative (BMI)
P.O. Box 90363
Nashville, Tennessee 37209

Lunacy (BMI)
5836 David Ave.
Los Angeles, California 90034

M

M, M&M

Maanami (ASCAP)
see EMI-April Music Inc.

Magnetic Force (ASCAP)

Magnified (ASCAP)
see WB Music Corp.

Maim That Tune (ASCAP)

Major Bob Music (ASCAP)
1109 17th Avenue South
Nashville, Tennessee 37212

Make It Big (ASCAP)
c/o WB Music
9000 Sunset Blvd.
Los Angeles, California 90069

Malaco Music Co. (BMI)
P.O. Box 9287
Jackson, Mississippi 39206

Man Woman Together Now Music (BMI)
see Irving Music Inc.

Mantanzas Music (ASCAP)
see Virgin Music, Inc.

Marissa (ASCAP)
see California Phase Music

Biz Markie (ASCAP)
see WB Music Corp.

Marledge (ASCAP)
813 18th Ave. South
Nashville, Tennessee 37203

Mick Mars (BMI)
9255 Sunset Blvd.
Los Angeles, California 90069

Matt-Black (ASCAP)
see EMI-April Music Inc.

Mattie Ruth (ASCAP)
1010 16th Ave. South
Nashville, Tennessee 37212

Maypop Music (BMI)
Att: Maggie Cavender
803 18th Avenue, S.
Nashville, Tennessee 37203

MCA, Inc. (ASCAP)
c/o Mr. John McKellen
445 Park Avenue
New York, New York 10022

MCA Music (ASCAP)
Division of MCA Inc.
445 Park Avenue
New York, New York 10022

McGuinn (BMI)
c/o Roger McGuinn
P.O. Box 5437
Indian Rocks Beach, Florida 33535

Metal Machine Music
Address Unavailable

Midsummer Music (ASCAP)
see EMI-April Music Inc.

List of Publishers

Mille Miglia Musique (ASCAP)
641 South Palm St., Ste. D
La Habra, California 90631

Millhouse (BMI)

Mine Music, Ltd. (ASCAP)
c/o S. Weintraub
271 Madison Avenue
New York, New York 10016

Miss Bessie Music (ASCAP)
9247 Alden Drive
Los Angeles, California 90210

Miss Boo (BMI)
11084 Culver Blvd.
Culver City, California 90230

Mr. Bolton's Music (BMI)
c/o David Feinstein
120 E. 34th Street, Suite 7F
New York, New York 10011

Moline Valley (ASCAP)
2132 No. Tremont
Chicago, Illinois 60614

Monsari (ASCAP)

Morganactive Music (ASCAP)
c/o Dennis Morgan
1800 Grand Avenue
Nashville, Tennessee 37212

Motherman (ASCAP)
see EMI-Blackwood Music Inc.

Motley Crue (BMI)
see WB Music Corp.

MPL Communications Inc. (ASCAP)
c/o Lee Eastman
39 W. 54th Street
New York, New York 10019

Muffin Stuffin (BMI)
3624 Fir
San Diego, California 92104

Murrah (BMI)
1025 16th Ave. South, Ste. 102
P.O. Box 121623
Nashville, Tennessee 37212

Music by Candlelight

Music Corp. of America (BMI)
see MCA, Inc.

Music Ridge (ASCAP)

Music Sales Corp. (ASCAP)
24 E. 22nd Street
New York, New York 10010

Must Be Marvelous

Muy Bueno Music (BMI)
1000 18th Street, S.
Nashville, Tennessee 37212

My Choy (BMI)
c/o Copyright Management Inc.

My My Music (ASCAP)
Address unavailable

Mya-T (BMI)
see Saja Music

Mycenae Music Publishing Co. (ASCAP)
c/o Cohen & Steinhart
Att: Martin Cohen
6430 Sunset Blvd., Suite 1500
Los Angeles, California 90028

N

Nelana Music (BMI)
c/o Fishbach & Fishbach
1925 Century Park, E., Suite 1260
Los Angeles, California 90067

Nemesis

Ness, Nitty & Capone (ASCAP)
see EMI-April Music Inc.

New Jersey Underground
see Bon Jovi Publishing

New Kids (ASCAP)
11945 Riverside Drive
No. Hollywood, California 91607

Randy Newman Music (ASCAP)
c/o Gelfand, Rennert & Feldman
1880 Century Park, E., Suite 900
Los Angeles, California 90067

Next Decade

Nia (BMI)
c/o Michael Snaders
9833 S. Calhoun
Chicago, Illinois 60617

Frank Nitty (ASCAP)
see EMI-April Music Inc.

No K. O. Music (ASCAP)
c/o Bug Music Group
6777 Hollywood Blvd., 9th Fl.
Hollywood, California 90028

No Tomato (ASCAP)
see WB Music Corp.

Notable Music Co., Inc. (ASCAP)
Cy Coleman Enterprises
200 W. 54th Street
New York, New York 10019

O

O-Tex (BMI)
see Muy Bueno Music

Of the Fire Music (ASCAP)
c/o Daniel Zanes
117 Pembroke Street
Boston, Massachusetts 02118

O.K. Paul Music

On the Move
Address Unavailable

Onid Music (BMI)
see Island Music

Open Window Music Co. (BMI)
see WB Music Corp.

Otherwise Publishing (ASCAP)
c/o Mark Tanner
1009 Ninth Street, Suite 3
Santa Monica, California 90403

P

Pac Jam Publishing (BMI)
c/o Marty Wekser
3575 Cahuenga Blvd. West, Ste. 415
Los Angeles, California

Martin Page (ASCAP)
c/o WB Music
9000 Sunset Blvd.
Los Angeles, California 90069

Page Three (BMI)

Panchin (BMI)
c/o Alan N. Skiena
200 W. 57th Street
New York, New York 10019

Pasta

Pax Music (ASCAP)
see Cherry Lane Music Co., Inc.

Peach Pie (ASCAP)
114 Knoll Drive
Blackwood, New Jersey 08012

Peer-Southern Organization
1740 Broadway
New York, New York 10019

Pennachio

Pillarview

Pink Pig Music (BMI)
c/o Funky But Music
P.O. Box 1770
Hendersonville, Tennessee 37075

Point Barrow (BMI)

Poison Brisket Music (BMI)
see Bug Music

Polygram International (ASCAP)
see Polygram Music Publishing Inc.

Polygram Music Publishing Inc. (ASCAP)
Att: Brian Kelleher
c/o Polygram Records Inc.
810 Seventh Avenue
New York, New York 10019

Polygram Songs (BMI)
810 Seventh Avenue
New York, New York 10019

Pookie Bear (ASCAP)
P.O. Box 121242
Nashville, Tennessee 37212

Portrait (ASCAP)
see Tree Publishing Co., Inc.

List of Publishers

Post Oak (BMI)
see Tree Publishing Co., Inc.

PRI Music (ASCAP)
810 7th Ave.
New York City, New York 10019

PRI Songs

Priestman (ASCAP)
see Virgin Music, Inc.

Probullio Publishing (BMI)
see EMI-Blackwood Music Inc.

Progeny Music (BMI)
c/o David Cohen
Plant, Cohen & Co.
10900 Wilshire Blvd., Suite 900
Los Angeles, California 90024

Promostraat

PSO Ltd. (ASCAP)
see Peer-Southern Organization

Pubhowyalike (BMI)
c/o A Train Mgmt
Attn: Tambre Bryant
1615 Broadway, Ste. 410
Oakland, California 94604

Pursuit of Tunes

Q

QPM

Quackenbush Music, Ltd. (ASCAP)
c/o Gelfand, Rennert & Feldman
Att: Babbie Green
1880 Century Park, E., No. 900
Los Angeles, California 90067

Queen Music Ltd. (BMI)
see Beechwood Music Corp.

R

R Mode Music

Eddie Rabbitt Music Publishing (BMI)
c/o Gelfand, Rennert & Feldman
7 Music Circle N.
Nashville, Tennessee 37203

Radical Dichotomy (BMI)

Rambush (ASCAP)
see Almo Music Corp.

Ranch Rock (ASCAP)
see WB Music Corp.

Reach Songs (ASCAP)
26 W. 71st. St.
New York, New York 10022

Really Useful Group (ASCAP)
see Screen Gems-EMI Music Inc.

Realsongs (ASCAP)
Address Unavailable

Reata Publishing Inc. (ASCAP)
9000 Sunset Blvd.
Los Angeles, California 90069

Red Brazos (BMI)
see Howlin' Hits Music

Red Guitar Blue Music (BMI)
Box 644
Northampton, Massachusetts 01061

Red Instructional Music (ASCAP)
c/o David B. Cole
134 Ninth Avenue, No. 5F
New York, New York 10011

Revelation Music Publishing Corp. (ASCAP)
Tommy Valando Publishing Group Inc.
1270 Avenue of the Americas
Suite 2110
New York, New York 10020

REW (ASCAP)
see WB Music Corp.

Rhyme Syndicate (ASCAP)
2825 Dunbar Drive
Riverside, California 92503

Rich McBitch Music (BMI)
see Virgin Music, Inc.

Rilting Music Inc. (ASCAP)
see Fiddleback Music Publishing Co., Inc.

Robi-Roy (ASCAP)
see Virgin Music, Inc.

Rodsongs (ASCAP)
see Kidada Music Inc.

Ronestone

Rossaway (BMI)

RSK

Ruthless Attack Muzick (ASCAP)
23126 Locust Ridge Circle
Valencia, California 91354

Rutland Road (ASCAP)
see Almo Music Corp.

S

Saja Music (BMI)
c/o Le Frak Ent.
40 W. 57th Street
New York, New York 10019

Salski (BMI)
c/o Sal Abbatiello
P.O. Box 219
Yonkers, New York 10710

J.D. Sandefer

Sapsucker

Sarapis (ASCAP)
see Selessongs

Savage Conquest Music (ASCAP)
332 Madison Drive, #3R
Hoboken, New Jersey 07030

Scaramanga Music (ASCAP)
c/o William A. Coben, Esq.
2029 Century Park, E., No. 2600
Los Angeles, California 90067

Scarlet Moon Music (BMI)
P.O. Box 120555
Nashville, Tennessee 37212

Jason Scheff (BMI)
see EMI-Blackwood Music Inc.

Don Schlitz Music (ASCAP)
P.O. Box 120594
Nashville, Tennessee 37212

Screen Gems-EMI Music Inc. (BMI)
6255 Sunset Blvd., 12th Fl.
Hollywood, California 90028

Second Hand Songs (BMI)
c/o Interior Music
Attn: Margo Matthews
9229 Sunset Blvd., Ste. 183
Los Angeles, California 90069

See the Light (BMI)
see Cherry Lane Music Co., Inc.

Selessongs (ASCAP)
9710 Zelzah Avenue, No. 101
Northridge, California 91325

Serenity Manor (ASCAP)
see Chappell & Co., Inc.

Seventh Son (ASCAP)
Address Unavailable

Seventh Son Music Inc. (ASCAP)
c/o Glen Campbell Enterprises Ltd.
10351 Santa Monica Blvd,, Suite 300
Los Angeles, California 90025

Sikki Nixx (BMI)
9255 Sunset Blvd.
Los Angeles, California 90069

Silver Fiddle (ASCAP)
c/o Segel & Goldman Inc.
9200 Sunset Blvd., Suite 1000
Los Angeles, California 90069

Silverline Music, Inc. (BMI)
329 Rockland Road
Hendersonville, Tennessee 37075

Paul Simon Music (BMI)
1619 Broadway
New York, New York 10019

Sindrome (BMI)
see EMI-Blackwood Music Inc.

Singletree Music Co., Inc. (BMI)
815 18th Avenue, S.
Nashville, Tennessee 37213

Six Continents Music Publishing Inc.
8304 Beverly Blvd.
Los Angeles, California 90048

Skyyzoo Songs (ASCAP)
147-15 230 Street
Rosedale, New York 11413

List of Publishers

Slap Me One Music (ASCAP)
c/o Avant Garde
Attn: M. Matthews
9229 Sunset Blvd., Suite 311
Los Angeles, California 90069

Sleeping Bag Music
Rt. 1, Box 487
West Hurley, New York 12491

Slik Star (ASCAP)
see Willesden Music, Inc.

Small Hope Music (BMI)
see Virgin Music, Inc.

Snowden/Hannibal

Songs of Grand Coalition Malaco Music
(BMI)
see Malaco Music Co.

Songs of Logic (BMI)
see Intersong, USA Inc.

Songways Service Inc.
10 Columbus Circle, Suite 1406
New York, New York 10019

Special Rider Music (ASCAP)
P.O. Box 860, Cooper Sta.
New York, New York 10276

Mark Spiro (BMI)
see Screen Gems-EMI Music Inc.

Bruce Springsteen Publishing (ASCAP)
c/o Jon Landau Management, Inc.
Att: Barbara Carr
136 E. 57th Street, No. 1202
New York, New York 10021

Stage & Screen Music Inc. (BMI)
see Unichappell Music Inc.

Stage-Screen Music, Inc. (BMI)
c/o Careers Music, Inc.
Att: Mr. Billy Meshel
8370 Wilshire Blvd.
Beverly Hills, California 90211

Stanley World

Stansbury (BMI)
14613 Tiara St.
Van Nuys, California 91401

Stanton's Gold (BMI)
see Island Music

Maurice Starr Music (ASCAP)
see EMI-April Music Inc.

Stephanie

Stevie Ray Songs (ASCAP)
see Bug Music

Stone Agate Music Corp. (BMI)
6255 Sunset Blvd.
Hollywood, California 90028

Stone City Music (ASCAP)
c/o Gross, Shuman, Brizdle
Laub, Gilfillan P.C.
2600 Main Place Tower
Buffalo, New York 14202

Stone Diamond Music Corp. (BMI)
6255 Sunset Blvd., Suite 1600
Dept. 4-7566
Los Angeles, California 90028

Story Songs Ltd. (ASCAP)
Marshall, Morris, Powell & Silfen
130 W. 57th Street
New York, New York 10019

Strong Island (ASCAP)
8109 Vermeer Place
Philadelphia, Pennsylvania 19153

Tom Sturges (ASCAP)
see Chrysalis Music Corp.

Sugarbiscuit (ASCAP)
c/o HEG Music Group
2712
Beverly Hills, California 90213

Sun Face

Sun Mare Music Publishing (BMI)
50 Music Square West, Ste. 503
Nashville, Tennessee 37203

Sure Fire Music Co., Inc.
60 Music Square, W.
Nashville, Tennessee 37203

Al B. Sure International (ASCAP)
P.O. Box 8075
Englewood, New Jersey 07631

Swag Song Music (ASCAP)
5 Bigelow Street
Cambridge, Massachusetts 02129

Swallowfork Music, Inc. (ASCAP)
453 Capri Road
Cocoa Beach, Florida 32931

Keith Sweat (ASCAP)
Address Unavailable

Sweet Cyanide (BMI)
see Willesden Music, Inc.

T

Tabraylah (ASCAP)
2029 Century Park East, #1700
Los Angeles, California 90067

Taurus Music

Paul Taylor (BMI)

TCF (ASCAP)
see WB Music Corp.

Ten Ten Tunes (ASCAP)
1010 16th Ave. South
Nashville, Tennessee 37212

Texas City (BMI)
c/o Backstreet
90 Universal City
Universal City, California 91608

Texas Wedge (ASCAP)
11 Music Square East
Nashville, Tennessee 37212

Theobalds (ASCAP)
see Polygram Music Publishing Inc.

They Might Be Giants Music (ASCAP)
232 N. Fifth Street
Brooklyn, New York 11211

Third Story Music Inc. (BMI)
6430 Sunset Blvd., Suite 1500
Los Angeles, California 90028

Three Headed (BMI)
see PRI Music

Threesome Music
1801 Avenue of the Stars, Suite 911
Los Angeles, California 90067

Tionna Music
see Controversy Music

Tol Muziek

Tomata du Plenti (ASCAP)
see Bug Music

Tony! Toni! Tone! (ASCAP)
see PRI Music

Topless (ASCAP)
see Chrysalis Music Corp.

Tracye One (BMI)
see Island Music

Tranquility Base Songs (ASCAP)
c/o Tom Shannon
5101 Whitesett Avenue
Studio City, California 91607

Tree Publishing Co., Inc. (BMI)
P.O. Box 1273
Nashville, Tennessee 37203

Tri-Chappell Music Inc. (ASCAP)
see Chappell & Co., Inc.

Trio Music Co., Inc. (BMI)
1619 Broadway
New York, New York 10019

Trippland (BMI)

TRO-Cromwell Music Inc. (ASCAP)
10 Columbus Circle
New York, New York 10019

True North Music (ASCAP)
see Almo Music Corp.

Tuff Cookie (BMI)

Tunes-R-Us (ASCAP)
218 S. 16th St., Ste. 300
Philadelphia, Pennsylvania 19103

Turkishman

Turnout Brothers Publishing Co. (ASCAP)
c/o Lawrence Lighter, Esq.
3 E. 54th Street, Suite 1200
New York, New York 10022

2 Kids (ASCAP)
see BMG Music

List of Publishers

Two-Sons Music (ASCAP)
   44 Music Square, W.
   Nashville, Tennessee 37203

Two Tuff-Enuff Publishing (BMI)
   6042 Bellingham Drive
   Castro Valley, California 94552

David Tyson

U

Ultrawave (ASCAP)

Unichappell Music Inc. (BMI)
   810 Seventh Avenue, 32nd Fl.
   New York, New York 10019

Unicity Music, Inc. (ASCAP)
   c/o MCA Music
   445 Park Avenue
   New York, New York 10022

United Lion Music Inc. (BMI)
   c/o United Artists Corp.
   729 Seventh Avenue
   New York, New York 10019

Upala (BMI)
   see Hamstein Music

V

Varry White Music (ASCAP)
   7471 Melrose Avenue, No. 25
   Los Angeles, California 90046

Velle International (ASCAP)
   see EMI-April Music Inc.

Vermal (BMI)
   see EMI-Blackwood Music Inc.

Vertim

Virgin Music, Inc. (ASCAP)
   Att: Ron Shoup
   43 Perry Street
   New York, New York 10014

Virgin Songs (BMI)
   see Virgin Music, Inc.

Vision of Love Songs Inc. (BMI)
   Padell, Nadell, Fine, Weinberger
   1775 Broadway
   7th Fl.
   New York City, New York 10019

Voltone (BMI)

Vomit God (ASCAP)
   see Cherry Lane Music Co., Inc.

W

Waifersongs Ltd. (ASCAP)
   c/o Michael C. Lesser, Esq.
   225 Broadway, Suite 1915
   New York, New York 10007

Warner Brothers, Inc. (ASCAP)
   9000 Sunset Blvd.
   Los Angeles, California 90069

Warner-Chappell Music (ASCAP)
   see WB Music Corp.

Warner-Elektra-Asylum Music Inc. (BMI)
   1815 Division Street
   Nashville, Tennessee 37203

Warner-Tamerlane Publishing Corp. (BMI)
   see WB Music Corp.

Warner/Unichappell

Mervyn Warren (BMI)

Waterwind (BMI)
   see EMI-Blackwood Music Inc.

WB Music Corp. (ASCAP)
   c/o Warner Brothers, Inc.
   Att: Leslie E. Bider
   9000 Sunset Blvd., Penthouse
   Los Angeles, California 90069

Webo Girl Music/WB Music Corp. (ASCAP)
   c/o Rubin, Baum, Levin, Cowstant,
   Friedman
   645 Fifth Avenue
   New York, New York 10022

We'll Do You (ASCAP)
   see Zomba Enterprises, Inc.

David Werner (ASCAP)
   see EMI-April Music Inc.

Cheryl Wheeler Music (ASCAP)
see Bug Music

Whistling Moon Traveler (BMI)
see Irving Music Inc.

Whole Nine Yards (ASCAP)
see WB Music Corp.

Wild Crusade (ASCAP)
see Chappell & Co., Inc.

Wild Gator Music (ASCAP)
see Gomace Music, Inc.

Wild Honey Publishing Co. (ASCAP)
1250 S. Arlington, #4
Los Angeles, California 90019

David N. Will (ASCAP)
see Willin' David

Willesden Music, Inc. (BMI)
c/o Zomba House
1348 Lexington Avenue
New York, New York 10028

Mentor Williams (ASCAP)
1800 Grand Ave.
Nashville, Tennessee 37212

Willin' David (BMI)
1205 16th Avenue, S.
Nashville, Tennessee 37212

Wilphill (ASCAP)
see EMI-April Music Inc.

Windswept Pacific (ASCAP)
4450 Lakeside Dr., Ste. 200
Burbank, California 91505

Winston Kae (BMI)

With Any Luck Music (BMI)
c/o Randy Sharp
14321 Valerio Street
Van Nuys, California 91405

Elliott Wolff Music (ASCAP)

Wrensong (ASCAP)
1229 17th Avenue, N.
Nashville, Tennessee 37212

W.S. (BMI)

X

XTC

Y

You'll Be Sorry

Your Mother's (BMI)
see Def American Songs

Yuck Music

Johnny Yuma (BMI)
c/o Fitzgerald Hartley Co.
7250 Beverly Blvd.
Los Angeles, California 90036

Z

Zappo Music (ASCAP)
Att: Bruce R. Hornsby
16815 Hartland Street
Van Nuys, California 91406

Zen of Iniquity (ASCAP)
c/o MFC Management
1428 S. Sherbourne Drive
Los Angeles, California 90035

Zero Productions (BMI)
c/o Clog Holdings
3300 Warner Blvd.
Burbank, California 91501

Zevon Music Inc. (BMI)
c/o Jess Morgan & Co., Inc.
6420 Wilshire Blvd., 19th Fl.
Los Angeles, California 90048

Zomba Enterprises, Inc. (BMI)
c/o Zomba House
1348 Lexington Avenue
New York, New York 10128

ZTT Records Ltd.